REAL
RAILWAY
TALES

REAL RAILWAY TALES

GEOFF BODY AND BILL PARKER

The
History
Press

First published 2014

The History Press
The Mill, Brimscombe Port
Stroud, Gloucestershire, GL5 2QG
www.thehistorypress.co.uk

British Library Cataloguing in Publication Data.
A catalogue record for this book is available from the British Library.

ISBN 978 0 7509 5635 2
Typesetting and origination by The History Press
Printed in Great Britain

CONTENTS

INTRODUCTION, SOURCES AND ACKNOWLEDGEMENTS

The truth may or may not be stranger than fiction, but it can certainly be strange, humorous, dramatic, and fascinating. At least, that is what the editor and compiler have again found in putting together this, the third book of stories from railway careers of every sort and function. We also have a strong conviction that, however interesting the infrastructure of the large and varied railway business may be, the real heart of this great industry lies in its people, the complex jobs they have occupied and the dedicated way they have carried them out.

The book contains a few experiences of our own but, for the most part, relies on the enthusiasm and effort of its generous contributors. Stalwarts from previous volumes, like Bryan Stone and Philip Benham, have once more done us proud and we have been able to add the prolific Willesden area tales of Chris Blackman, and those of Terry Worrall. Jim Dorward and Hugh Gould have again kept Scotland in the picture, David Jagoe has provided the Welsh entries, Theo Steel has sent further copy on slightly way-out subjects and Margaret Ritchie has recorded an astounding journey from trainee typist to chairman's personal assistant. The full list of contributors is shown with the contents details and we are extremely grateful to each and every one.

Our sources are solely these valued contributors, many of whom have also supplied illustrations. These are acknowledged with the captions, all the others coming from the Geoffrey Body Collection.

We hope readers will enjoy these tales as much as they clearly did those in *Signal Box Coming Up, Sir* and *Along Different Lines*.

Authors' note: Sadly, Margaret Ritchie died between submitting her contribution and publication of this book.

GLOSSARY

ALA	Angleterre-Lorraine-Alsace, providing ferry services between Dover and Dunkerque
AMI	Area Movements Inspector
ASLEF	Associated Society of Locomotive Engineers and Firemen
ATOC	Association of Train Operating Companies
BR	British Rail or British Railways
BRB	British Railways Board
BRIS	British Railways Infrastructure Services
C&D	Collection and Delivery
CMEE	Chief Mechanical & Electrical Engineer
C&W	Carriage & Wagon department
Dc	Direct electrical current
DB	The German railway system
DCC	Deputy Chief Controller
DI	District Inspector
DMU	Diesel multiple unit
DOS	District or Divisional Operating Superintendent
DTM	District or Divisional Traffic Manager
DTSO	District Traffic Superintendent's Office
ECML	East Coast Main Line
EMU	Electric multiple unit
EPS	European Passenger Services
ER	Eastern Region of British Railways
ETS	Electric traction supply
GCR	Great Central Railway
GER	Great Eastern Railway
GNR	Great Northern Railway
GWR	Great Western Railway

H&B	Hull & Barnsley Railway
HMRI	Her Majesty's Railway Inspectorate
Hopper wagon	Wagon designed for bottom discharge by gravity
HST	High Speed Train
ISO	Container built to international standards
L&M	Liverpool & Manchester Railway
LMR	London Midland Region of British Railways
LMSR	London Midland & Scottish Railway
L&NWR	London & North Western Railway
LNER	London & North Eastern Railway
M&GN	Midland & Great Northern Railway
Midland	The Midland Railway or London Midland Region
MSLR	Manchester Sheffield & Lincolnshire Railway
On the cushions	Travelling as a passenger
NS	Netherlands Railway System
NUR	National Union of Railwaymen
PWI	Permanent Way Inspector
RMT	Rail, Maritime and Transport Workers Union
SNCF	French railway system
SNCB	Belgian railway system
SR	Southern Railway or Southern Region of British Railways
SRA	Strategic Rail Authority
Tippler wagon	Wagon designed for side tipping to unload
Time interval	Control of trains by signalmen when normal communications are lost
WCML	West Coast Main Line
WR	Western Region of British Railways

COLD RELIEF AT DERBY

When Philip Benham started his railway career he was told that he would 'learn best on the job' which proved very true, but sometimes quite uncomfortable

The transition from school to work can be quite a shock to the system. For me it came on 4 September 1968 when I started work in the Nottingham Division of British Railways as a 'traffic student'. This was a training programme for school leavers aimed at giving a general grounding in railway work. For those who did well there was the prospect of moving up the promotional ladder, or even management training, although nothing was guaranteed.

Day one started with a welcome from 'Colonel' Gardiner, the redoubtable Nottingham Divisional Manager, an encounter that lasted all of two minutes – such interviews became renowned for their brevity in which hapless trainees discovered the error of their ways. Then it was off to Derby, where I was placed under the wing of Area Manager Harry Potts and told that I would learn best as a relief clerk covering whatever job needed doing.

First was a spell as assistant controller in 'A' signal box, situated under the footbridge in the middle of Derby Midland station. Steam traction had just ended, but in other respects Derby was still very much the old railway. 'A Box' controlled the train movements through the station, including those through the crossovers which switched trains between platforms – useful if vehicles were blocking one end of one of these. It was relatively modern, having replaced an older signal box when the station was rebuilt around 1953 after war damage. To the north and south, Derby Station North and London Road Junction boxes controlled entrance to the station. Further north still, Derby Junction box routed trains 'round the corner' to Derby South Junction and Chaddesden Sidings, while Derby North Junction controlled the third side of the triangle from Chaddesden. Within a mile of Derby station there were no less than ten manual signal boxes. In less than a year they would all be gone, replaced by the new Derby Power Signal Box. 'A Box' would survive as an inspector's office, and today looks to be the only bit of the 1950s station still standing.

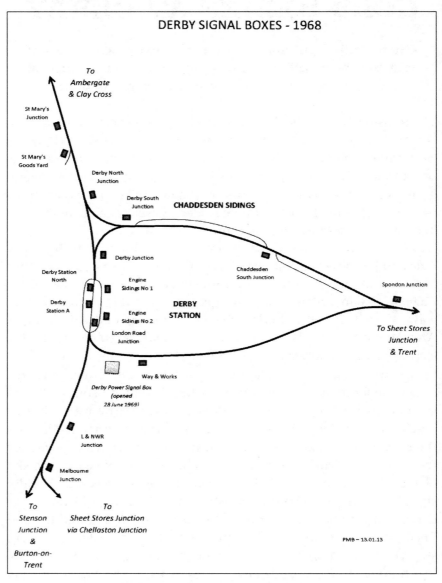

The routes and signal boxes at Derby in 1968. (Philip Benham)

The assistant controller's job was to keep local signal boxes advised about the running of trains, these ranging as far out as Burton-on-Trent, Clay Cross and Trent. This was important so that signalmen knew whether or not they had sufficient margin to run a slower freight train without delaying higher category passenger and parcels services. They would soon shout if a report was missed as a 'please explain' could follow if an express was delayed.

I was given a week on each shift. The work was 'round the clock' so the joys of night work were experienced for the first time. (Why does time pass so much more slowly between 3 and 5 a.m.?) The main tools of the trade were 'roneoed' (printed) sheets showing the scheduled passing and arrival times for trains through the area, on to which the actual times were recorded, and a large telephone concentrator for receiving and making calls. Most signal boxes were on 'omnibus' telephone circuits, which meant that everyone could listen to all conversations. Individual signal boxes were called using ring codes and the trick was to develop 'controller's ear' to listen to several conversations at once and never miss hearing your own ring code.

With over 200 trains a day the job was always busy, but the real fun came when things went wrong.

I arrived one morning to find all the signalling to the north was out of order due to the theft of signalling cable and trains were being worked under the 'time interval' system. A hectic morning followed, with trains queuing up as the morning peak progressed, but the Signal & Telegraph lads were on the job and by midday all was back to normal. The repair team duly retired for a well-earned brew only to find that, while in their mess hut, the thieves had returned and stolen the new cable! The problem of cable theft that dogs the modern railway is by no means new.

After a few months I was moved to other work and covered all sorts of jobs, from booking clerk to train announcer. This first winter of work included a particularly cold spell which gave me what I still regard as my worst ever job, that of 'sheeting' parcels. This was done at Derby St Andrews, adjoining the passenger station and originally a goods depot for the London & North Western Railway, but by now given over to parcels' traffic. Sheeting involved recording on to large sheets details of received parcels, including the delivery address, as a porter sorted them into road delivery rounds. The sheets would then be used by the

In wintry conditions, a Nottingham-bound diesel multiple unit passes Derby Junction signal box under clear signals. (Philip Benham)

delivery van drivers to plan their rounds and obtain delivery signatures. The mail order business was in full swing at this time and made up the bulk of the hundreds of parcels received off the overnight trains.

This was night work and, with temperatures that winter often sub-zero, frozen fingers made it all but impossible to hold a pen (or, more often, a pencil as pens failed in the cold), let alone write legibly. The mess facilities were basic, but at least were warm and the tea always hot. As the minutes to the next break ticked slowly by, the mess-room image danced in the imagination like some Shangri-La. For years to come the names of the mail order companies like Grattan and Littlewoods were enough to send a shudder of recollection down my spine.

It was a relief when I was transferred to learn the job of goods guards' clerk at Chaddesden Sidings. Once a major marshalling yard, Chaddesden's role had reduced following closure of the Midland route to Manchester a few months before, but several trains still called and a couple of shunting engines were kept occupied.

The clerk worked in the yardmaster's office, with the main task being the rostering of guards to specific trains. A good roster clerk requires skills that must rank with those needed by any foreign diplomat. Tact, good humour, fairness and, above all, powers of persuasion, are among the vital attributes. Since I was covering the job for only a short time, how the guards really felt about 'this young whippersnapper' I can only imagine, but I was treated with unfailing good humour and kindness. As everywhere, there were some real characters. One, Guard Kirk, still proudly wore his Wyvern cap badge, reflecting the fact that he had started work on the Midland Railway. Another, who had worked on the Settle & Carlisle line back in the war, still claimed to 'sign the road' to Glasgow – a dubious claim because you were supposed to work over a route every six months to retain route knowledge.

I was not yet done with the cold. My time at Chaddesden corresponded with the worst of the winter snow. The yard supervisor thought I should learn about clearing snow from points and signals, so yet another cold job. A device I became familiar with was a steam lance, used for thawing snow and ice, and fitted to the locomotive steam pipe. This worked well initially, but in sub-zero temperatures the steam could rapidly condense and freeze, sometimes leaving more ice than before.

After eighteen months I moved on to the divisional office. Learning on the job had proved invaluable and I have cause to thank the many railwaymen and women who gave me such a good grounding.

LIGHTER MOMENTS

Among the daily catalogue of serious railway decisions and actions, Jim Gibbons experienced a few lighter moments

PURSER'S URGENT MESSAGE

My first 'outside' appointment was as summer season assistant at the Channel port of Folkestone. Luckily, I was warned by a previous occupant of a trap which might be set for an unwary newcomer. A member of the station staff would say to the new manager that the purser of the ferry lying alongside needed to speak to the station manager urgently.

The manager would then respond by hastening to board the ship and look for the purser. On finding him eventually and asking what he wanted, the railway representative would be told, 'I'm not looking for you; never have been.'

On making his way back to the gangway wondering what it was all about, the hapless manager would then see the ferry was, by this time, on its way to France. On his return some hours later, his boss would want to know where the hell he had been all day!

THE CHEF'S MIXED GRILL

My first 'real' operating job was the preparation of the weekly engineering works notice, known on the Southern as the 'P/EW'. This involved a weekly visit to the district civil engineer's office to collect the forthcoming track possession requests and agree the previous week's possessions, which had been published as a draft notice.

The office concerned was housed in 1940s wooden huts and, being totally self-sufficient, included a canteen, which I used. This was run by two people who, whilst looking like platelayers (i.e. tough macho types), produced very good meals. However, while 'learning the job' with my predecessor, I was strongly advised not to try the mixed grill.

Several weeks later, I was in the lunch queue when somebody ordered the said mixed grill. The 'chef' reached upwards and grasped the handle of a huge frying pan on the top of a cupboard. Immediately and dramatically a cat, which was curled up, fast asleep and out of sight, leaped out and made its escape. I also had quite an escape!

THE DAY WAR BROKE OUT

At one time, one of my divisional inspectors had had a previous career in the army and was on the reserve list when the Falkland Islands were invaded. He was a little concerned that he might be recalled for military service and one of the deputy chief controllers (DCCs) knew this. At that time the uniform hat issue for station managers and inspectors was the traditional peaked cap with a large flat top, and the inspector in question was of a tall, thin build.

The control deputy put out a general call for 'Inspector X to contact the DCC urgently in respect of the Falklands conflict'. The inspector did so, fearing the worst, only to be advised that he was required for the conflict because 'he and his hat were required for service as a helicopter landing pad!'

KEEPING COSTS DOWN

Most railway offices operated a 'tea club' on a co-operative basis and relied on one person to buy the provisions and collect a weekly charge from the participants. One such club I belonged to was run by a very cost-conscious person, who kept meticulous accounts.

Because the office concerned worked a fair amount of overtime the 'Tea Master' circulated members, pointing out the financial implications of those working early and late making additional cups of tea. This must have seemed to someone a step too far, for when the tea club supremo arrived at work the next morning there was a length of string across the office with a host of used tea bags clipped to it 'drying'!

A SECOND VISIT

My first appointment as an area manager was in a South London area and one of my first actions was to tour the stations under my control. I was talking to the people working at one of these and was asked by one of the platform staff whether I would be around on the following day. I explained that with some thirty stations in the area, I could not visit them all on a daily basis.

'Oh,' my questioner replied, 'only I won't be around tomorrow. I'm having a "comp" day.'

A comp day was a day's compensatory time allowed away additional to the normal leave rostered and earned for working on a public holiday. The conversation then continued:

'Are you going somewhere nice?'

'I'm going to France.'

'Very nice. Have you been before?'

'Oh yes; and the last time they made us jump off the boat.'

'Good Lord! Jump off the boat? When was that?'

'1944.'

Talk about walking into it! I had just not seen that coming.

HIGHDYKE

Easton, Colsterworth, Stainby and Sproxton were not well-known railway locations, but Bryan Stone reveals something of their considerable activity and importance

Some 400yd north of the country end of Stoke Tunnel there are some gentle humps which the East Coast passenger will scarcely notice. This was once the connection to the Highdyke branch, a place of lonely legend, where many Grantham railwaymen wrestled with enormous traffic volumes, heavy gradients, elderly engines, single lines, and long hours, while their colleagues on the Pacifics were still doing the glamorous stuff along the main line. Today it's all gone, so this is a good place to remember days spent up there.

Grantham was a main line 'staging post' with station, shed and the Nottingham, Lincoln and Sleaford branches. The station and yard were

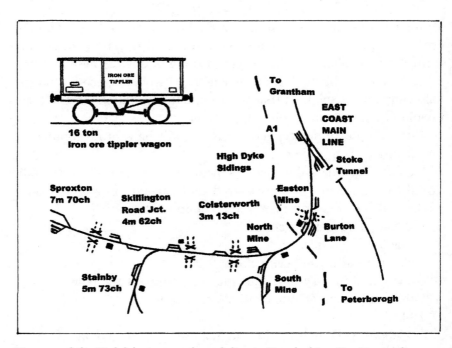

Diagram of the Highdyke iron ore branch line in Lincolnshire. (Jim Dorward)

alive in the 1950s with main line expresses, gleaming Pacifics and engine changing, and with branch trains slipping in and out. There was main line freight too, often fully braked high-speed services for fish, Scotch goods and so on. And several times a day, a travel-stained 2-8-0 would set off 'light engine' to the south, or lift a load of empty tipplers, and disappear away towards the Great North Road Bridge. Again, one of these great engines, a 3-cylinder Class O2, one of Gresley's lesser known masterpieces, would clatter through on a heavy load of ironstone, off north to the junction at Barkston and the Lincolnshire Wolds beyond.

Now, first, a confession: Grantham and Highdyke were not in my division, which stopped short just outside Grantham station. It was King's Cross territory, but that ironstone originating on the Highdyke branch was a pillar of our Frodingham steelworks business so I had been several times to look around, before Grantham shed closed and the steam workings stopped.

There was no station at Highdyke. The name of the signal box came from Ermine Street, the 'High Dyke' of the Roman road, crossed here on its way to Lincoln. The way to get there was on an

K3 2-6-0 locomotive No. 61829 heads an Up freight train past Highdyke signal box and sidings on the East Coast Main Line. (Bryan Stone)

A view from the brake van of a train of empty iron-ore wagons heading up the Highdyke–Stainby branch. (Bryan Stone)

engine or brake van. Remoteness – though it was only 4 miles south of Grantham – required seeking the cryptic entries in the Freight Working Timetable of the East Coast Main Line which showed 'EBV', i.e. engine and brake van, Grantham–Highdyke and back. These ran when the shifts changed, to carry shunters, guards and locomen. They were worked by anything convenient at Grantham shed, an L1 or A5 off the branches, for example, for the booked twelve minutes' ride. The pilot engines, those great O2s, ran up and down light or with brake vans, and a lift on a booked ironstone working was also possible.

So what was it all about? Britain's industry of coal and iron, and then steel, needed raw materials. One of these was iron ore, and iron-works were first built where it could be dug up; Frodingham, on the Doncaster–Grimsby route, was one such place. Since iron ore was to be found in many places in the Lincolnshire Wolds, there had been extensive mines, but it was often poor stuff, and varied in impurities. Before the First World War, demand for steel for ships and arma-ments, railways and construction had pushed the old ways aside and new huge steelworks were built. That, in turn, meant using more and

A trainload of iron ore nears Highdyke. The brake van has been detached and will run by gravity into a separate siding. (Bryan Stone)

better ironstone, brought from further away. Highdyke was in the business, for there nature had provided, under the hills about half-way from Grantham to Melton Mowbray, a huge deposit of siliceous iron ore rock. A branch to Stainby built in 1915 was extended with short branches by the Appleby-Frodingham Steel Company in 1916.

Names like Stainby, Sproxton and Colsterworth now became more familiar – great open mines where the steelworks' own locomotives served the shovels and gave loads to BR. These I saw being made into branch trains by the two pilots. You went up with a trip from Highdyke Yard, a place where shunting was ingeniously done mainly by train engines, pilots, and gravity, of which, on a hill and with steep gradients, there was a lot. By my time there was no branch timetable, the two pilots making trips as required, which meant being hard at it all day. Electric token operation was in use from Highdyke to Sproxton using Tyers No. 6 tablet working on the first section to Colsterworth and having a token exchange cabin on the final portion. The Stainby branch was worked under One Engine in Steam regulations, i.e. only one train was permitted on the branch at a time, although operational methods over the whole branch were modified from time to time. The pilot locomotives had tablet catchers, but they told me this was a menace and firemen preferred to exchange by hand.

The trip had its excitement. Trains were all loose coupled; I see from my notes that we took up thirty empties, some 200 tons, but the grade leaving the transfer sidings at Highdyke was 1 in 40, straight off the yard. The trick was to take a run from the empty sidings behind the box, go hell-for-leather for the bank and come out three-quarters of a mile later on a level plateau, at walking pace. This is beautifully caught, by the way, on a Transacord recording of that time.

From this point westwards, there was a see-saw of at worst 1 in 40, a lot of 1 in 60, all the way to Colsterworth Sidings and Skillington Road. Handling trains was an art, if the guard (and the train) were to survive without breaking things. That bank out of Highdyke was also a potential menace for breakaways, ending up next to the East Coast Main Line. In the other direction, the worst uphill was 1 in 60, but getting down the 1 in 40 with twelve wagons of ore, about 400 tons gross, was the issue. The Appendix to the Working Timetable gave instructions to stop at the Stop-Board above Highdyke, to pin down brakes, and uncouple the brake van. I noticed on different occasions that about half the brakes (six out of twelve wagons) were pinned down. The driver would bring the train into the loaded sidings, the van came down by gravity to an empty road, and there we were, ready for the next lot.

The loads were re-marshalled into full trains at Highdyke for the long haul, most to Frodingham, some to Stanton (Colwick motive power worked them) and one or two to Parkgate, Aldwarke and further afield. Booked loads left Highdyke in 1959, at 00.28, 03.42, 06.46, 20.36, 22.50; that is five booked trains, nearly 4,000 tons of ore, each weekday. In 1964, by which time they were diesel-hauled with a 'fitted head' (i.e. some train braking, Class 7*), there were six daily trains of ore to Barnetby for trip working to the steelworks. At Highdyke the trips on the branch were matched to the making up of the scheduled block trains, and also the supply of incoming empties. By the time I got there, the wagons were no longer hoppers, but 27-ton tipplers, a rudimentary steel bin on four wheels, but the springs and bearings gave away the fact that they were quite tough. Seeing them being loaded by excavator was not for the faint-hearted! Brakes were the classic side hand lever, pinned down as needed.

At Skillington Road Class O2 locomotive No. 63932 will draw its twelve loaded
tippler wagons on to the single line for the guard to drop his van on to the train by
gravity. (Bryan Stone)

Highdyke signal box was only a few feet from the busy East Coast
Main Line and the signalmen there certainly had their hands full.
They controlled the two-track access to Stoke Tunnel as well as dealing
with the conflicting movements of ironstone trains, mineral empties
and light engine movements. They virtually managed the movement
activity along the branch. This would all have been for under £10 a
week. But, the staff in places like this were always remarkable, planning moves ahead with all the skill of a seasoned chess player, and we
learned to respect them.

I saw all this when Highdyke was noisy, smoky, industrious and
the staff tired and hard-pressed, struggling with rain and wind, steep
hills, handbrakes, dirty fires and worn locomotive big ends, shunting
and pulling the levers, sending literally millions of tons every year to
the steelworks. About five and a half hours it took to Frodingham,
but often longer; another story is the level crossings in Lincoln where
the ironstone trains reversed, stopping the town traffic some ten times
a day, and filling the local papers with comment.

Scunthorpe and Frodingham received 2.8 million tons of iron-stone in 1955, but the works also dug as much locally in their own mines. They also received about 2.6 million tons of coal and coke. The Frodingham end I knew better.

The Achilles heel was, apart from the decline of the steel industry, that by 1960 the inefficiency of the rail movement was obvious; more than three-quarters of what was dug, shunted and hauled around was rock, coming out of the processing eventually as slag. Ores landed at Immingham, Swedish or South American, were over 70 per cent iron; Lincolnshire's was not. It had to end. The East Coast trains fly past now on plain track.

Geoff Body adds:

Bryan's words brought back my own memories of the Highdyke-Stainby branch. For a start I had a family connection as my father, who had started work on the railway at nearby Great Ponton in 1916 at the tender age of 13, became a fully fledged male clerk when he was later sent to Stainby. Now 18, his new rate of pay was £80 a year and for the first time was sufficient to cover the lodgings he had to take with one of the Stainby signalmen, a man Dad called 'quite a card'.

When the Highdyke branch became part of my own commercial responsibility as Freight Sales Officer for the King's Cross Division I made a visit there with District Inspector Peter Keys in May 1965. Peter had been a signalman at the small Skillington Road Junction box at the tender age of 17. He later wrote his own memories of the branch, including some disastrous experiments with snow clearance in the winter of 1946–47 using an aircraft jet engine strapped to a railway wagon. It certainly cleared the snow, but also set fire to anything combustible in the vicinity and blasted the track all over the place.

My trip from Highdyke was with a load of empties behind a Brush diesel. Approaching Colsterworth North sidings, the wagons were held on brakes on the slope down to the siding points while the diesel came off the front and moved into the siding itself. The points were then reset, the wagons allowed to run down the approach slope and up the other side of the dip and, again, braked there. The Brush then emerged from the siding to climb the approach slope and be reunited with the empties which made their second trip of the see-saw to rejoin it and finally be propelled back into the loading sidings.

The mining activity was intense and fascinating, mostly with a huge 25-ton grab removing the surface layer to allow smaller machines to lift the iron ore and load it ready for rail movements. Easton mine differed, and was an underground operation involving blasting out tunnels, pumping out the resultant sludge and then mining between adjacent shafts. Conveyors elevated the mined ore for the overhead loading of wagons at 600 tons an hour. Although ankle-deep in sludge at the tunnel face, I would not have missed this dramatic encounter with one of my freight client's business.

Bill Parker, too, had a responsibility for the Highdyke–Stainby line when he was the district inspector at Peterborough in the 1950s. Whereas some of his other obligatory branch line visits – to Ramsey, Fletton or Stamford – were quite restful, the Highdyke branch was a hive of activity, exciting and only saved from being dangerous by the professionalism of the railwaymen who worked there. Bill comments:

Despite the hair-raising shunting and train working arrangements on the severe gradients, I recall only one instance of a runaway during my tenure. Eight loaded wagons of ore collided and became derailed, producing a heaped mess of wagon parts and ore to be cleared up. It was on those occasions, particularly in remote areas, when the superb fry-ups in the breakdown vans were really appreciated!

QUICK THINKING AT WIMBLEDON

Theo Steel uses his grandfather's notes to describe the rather unusual beginning to an Indian potentate's visit

In 1925 the Maharaja of Jodhpur brought his household with him on a visit to this country, along with his fifty polo ponies. My grandfather was engaged by the Maharaja's bankers, Coutts, to manage the visit. Among his tasks was to prepare a house in Wimbledon ready for the party's arrival; no small task for it involved carrying out structural alterations to create a 'Zenana' – special quarters for those in purdah. Grandfather's 1974 written description of the arrival by train records:

> An early interest was the delivery of several coach-built motor cars supplied by Barker & Hooper.
>
> These consisted of a large Zenana saloon – yellow and black with large, blacked-out windows – several other Rolls Royces and a number of more modest staff cars.
>
> The day of arrival was Easter Saturday and the party travelled from Dover to Wimbledon by special train. The 'Concours d'Elegance' of limousines gathered for their arrival created such a crowd that the police sent the cars back to the house to return when the train had arrived.
>
> At this stage it was realised that no preparations had been made to convey the ladies in purdah from the train to the Zenana vehicle. Luckily there was an Austin Seven on site and the problem was solved by driving it repeatedly down the slope on to the platform and then back with the ladies crouched out of sight inside.

Apparently the Maharaja's party did the London 'season' and then went up to Inverlochy Castle by special sleeper train from King's Cross for some shooting in the autumn.

Despite, or perhaps because of, the novel solution to the Wimbledon problem my grandfather was engaged to work in Jodhpur for the Maharaja for the next twenty years, rising to become his finance minister. He did much travelling around the state in a private saloon and there is even a story that my grandmother journeyed in a cold bath in the coach to try to escape the worst of the heat!

A SMALL EMPIRE

In the 1970s one man looked after an isolated branch line that produced some valuable freight business and is remembered affectionately by both Geoff Body and Bill Parker

Increasingly throughout the 1960s and 1970s branch lines came under unfriendly scrutiny. There was growing pressure to get rid of both poorly laden passenger trains and of fringe goods services. Main line operation and block trainloads were the thing. It was in this commercial climate that I was asked to examine the Ramsey branch shortly after my appointment as Freight Sales Officer in the King's Cross Division. Having been to school in Peterborough and worked in that district, I knew where Ramsey was and understood the nature of the flat, fertile lands of Cambridgeshire and Norfolk, but not much more than that.

After a preliminary survey of the data on record, I caught a train to Peterborough, picked up an office car and headed out over Farcet Fen. A slight detour took me to the former branch line depot at St Mary's, but little remained there, although I knew that at one time traffic had arrived by barge for transfer to rail. I headed on to Ramsey North, the former Ramsey East station being closed, and was agreeably surprised by the activity apparent there. I got down to the job of seeing all I could and listening to what I was told. Subsequently, information from the local operating and commercial people, working and financial data were all garnered and I duly presented my conclusions at the beginning of 1965. The first paragraph of the report read:

> This freight-only branch line runs for a distance of five miles, 1,243yd from Holme, 7 miles south of Peterborough, to Ramsey North. It is single throughout and is operated under the one engine in steam regulations. There is a public siding at Ramsey St Mary's and three road level crossings on the branch, the gates being opened and closed by the train crews. There are no private sidings. Freight and Parcels C&D services in the area are provided by vehicles based on Peterborough North.

27

This straight, lonely single line of railway running through flat, agricultural scenery epitomised the Ramsey North branch. Here, at St Mary's in 1964, only a marooned goods shed and loading dock survive.

So much for setting the scene. Pages of detailed traffic information and costs followed, with the latter summarised in a phrase that read, 'total direct savings are not expected to exceed £6,000 per annum against total receipts at risk of £25,000.' I strongly recommended retention of the line, at least until the situation changed, especially if a plan to concentrate the coal traffic of a wide area on Whitemoor actually came to anything. My divisional manager, Dick Hardy, backed these findings and headquarters at Liverpool Street left Ramsey and those running things alone to get on with their useful activity.

Rail life does not always permit people to know the outcome of their actions, but I was more fortunate in this case. In 1967 *Rail News* reported on the Ramsey branch under the heading of 'One Man Who's Out for Trade'. It was a good piece, describing the work of foreman Eric Marshall, who not only dealt with all the inwards and outwards freight wagons, but was not above seeking out and persuading firms who might have potential for more business to use the railway. At the time the branch was forwarding large volumes of grain to Manchester and Birkenhead, receiving fertiliser – sometimes in bulk trainload quantities – for local distribution and taking in 4,000 tons of coal a year plus 239 wagons of Scottish seed potatoes. All this was dealt with by one man with the help of the diesel shunting locomotive and crew which worked the branch, plus a bit of track care from the maintenance people.

The Ramsey branch had long since lost its passenger trains, but the booking office was still functional and Eric also managed to find time to issue tickets to the local community for journeys they planned to make from Huntingdon or Peterborough.

Inevitably, the tide of rationalisation swept over this tenacious survivor of the Great Northern's branch miscellany, but at least I helped to give it eight extra years of useful and profitable life.

Bill Parker, too, remembers the Ramsey branch:

The Ramsey branch was the southernmost outpost of my empire as the Peterborough North-based district inspector in the 1950s. Ramsey itself was quite a busy little goods depot in a most pleasant market town. As the branch line was operated under 'One Engine in Steam' regulations, there was no signal box at Ramsey, but I nonetheless made a point of visiting as often as possible to check the shunting operations, re-examine the foreman in biennial rules and regulations, and check wagon records and demurrage.

Access was not easy; in fact it was an 'Away-Day' break for me, as Assistant District Operating Superintendent John Christopher jokingly, or sarcastically, told me! My favourite method of getting there was on a freight trip from and to New England marshalling yard. This, however, caused me to be 'wired-on' by the signalman at Holme signal box, thus preventing me from arriving as a surprise to the Ramsey staff. My journey was nonetheless most enjoyable, travelling on the engine or in the guards van! If I wanted to arrive without advance warning I could arrange a ride in a road cartage vehicle through the good offices of the Peterborough North goods agent, or with a local freight sales representative ... or even by bus. I had no car and it was too far to cycle! As a backstop, the Peterborough-based British Transport Police were most accommodating, with an arrangement to send a police car to pick me up in the event of an emergency elsewhere. Needless to say, this inevitably occurred once, resulting in a very fast ride with lights flashing and sirens *fortissimo*.

Apart from the work to be done, I do recall the delightful Ramsey market day and purchasing in season pheasants and other game ... with strict instructions from Chief Inspector Harry Beeby to buy some to deliver to him at our regular Thursday visit to the King's Cross district headquarters at Knebwoth! Away from the dynamics of the East Coast Main Line, this really was a branch to be 'lost' on, but it was nevertheless a contributing part of the railway and my brief was 'not to neglect Ramsey'.

SHOVE-HA'PENNY

Before his sad death, Alex Bryce, a contributor to our previous volumes, sent us this story, included here as a tribute to a fine man and able colleague

My early career in Scotland involved many years as a relief clerk and as a relief stationmaster working in four of the Scottish Region districts at Glasgow, Edinburgh, Burntisland and Aberdeen. As a result of this peripatetic experience I had worked at over 200 different stations throughout the region before I secured my first permanent appointment in a post in the staff section of the district traffic superintendent's office in Aberdeen.

The district traffic superintendent (DTS) at this time was J.W. Barr, a former senior staff officer of the North Eastern Region and a very competent, but rather autocratic, manager whose specialist experience and knowledge could make life at times difficult for the staff section personnel and in particular the chief staff clerk John K. Davidson.

There was in operation at that time a buzzer system between the superintendent and the staff section with one buzz for the chief staff clerk and four for me as the general dogsbody of the section. As a result of the short fuse the DTS appeared to work on, the chief staff clerk would normally respond within seconds to the buzzer, but was always in some dread as to why he had been summoned.

On one of the rare occasions when I was called to attend the DTS I inadvertently entered his room without knocking on the door and received an inevitable severe dressing-down from him. This unhappy experience lived with me for some time and on a future nervous occasion when leaving his room I found myself knocking on the inside of the door before passing out of the room!

The office closed at 5 p.m. but many of the staff, including myself, lived out of Aberdeen and certain trains to Royal Deeside, for example, did not leave until nearly six o'clock. Many of us had about an hour to put in after work and we formed a shove-ha'penny league, which was joined by staff from four of the other sections of the DTSO. We had particularly suitable desks for playing this game and, as it only involved three coins for each player and plasticine goal posts, it became a very popular pastime, with some of the players developing a high level of skill in scoring goals.

One evening, when we were enjoying a particularly exciting and perhaps a little noisy match between two experts, the DTS in person suddenly appeared in the rather crowded room, demanding to know what all the noise was about and why we were still present in the office after hours. We apologised for disturbing him and explained about the game we were playing, but he responded sharply by saying he knew what we were doing as he had played a similar type of game in the North East at Darlington in his early career days. He appeared to soften his manner, perhaps by recollections of former times, and insisted in trying out his skills, but not with any great success.

Later, the chief staff clerk was horrified when I confessed to him about the DTS's visit and he was sure he would receive criticism for his inadequate supervision. Perhaps not surprisingly, however, it was never mentioned and we continued our shove-ha'penny league quite a long time after the unexpected visit.

TICKETS, PLEASE

**Cases of reluctance to buy a ticket are not unusual, but
Area Manager Terry Worrall describes two unusual
outcomes**

A MALE CINDERELLA

As I was leaving an office on the island platform at Coventry station one summer afternoon in 1974, I was approached by the conductor of a Euston–Wolverhampton train, which was standing at the Down platform, who advised me that there was an abusive passenger in first class who refused to show his ticket, 'if he had one!' To avoid further delay I offered to help and we boarded the train and found the passenger, a young man with his feet on the opposite seat, albeit without shoes. I introduced myself; the young man was unimpressed and told me to 'get lost' or words to that effect.

I saw his shoes on the floor, picked them up and told him that he could collect them from Coventry station at his convenience. I then left the train promptly – as did he – following me on to the platform, swearing and cursing. The platform staff gave the 'right away' and the train departed. The offending passenger obviously disliked the prospect of turning up at Birmingham or Wolverhampton without shoes.

The platform staff had by that time called for the assistance of the British Transport Police, who arrived in the nick of time. The shoeless passenger was taken to the police office in his stockinged feet where he was asked to identify the shoes as being his, which he did, clearly discomfited by their absence. He was then escorted to the ticket office and duly purchased a ticket.

We chose not to take the matter further; we did smile though!

ROUGH JUSTICE

One winter evening in the early part of my tenure at Paddington as acting area manager during 1980, I chose to do a night shift, essentially to observe the extensive and very busy newspaper train working, which reached its peak from 12.30 a.m. to 3 a.m. I was accompanied by Wally Richards, the area operations manager, who was more than familiar with these workings having been at Paddington for several years. As ever, Wally was in full uniform suit and bowler hat!

Immediately before the arrival of the first wave of road vehicles, we chose to walk alongside the Penzance sleeping car train which was standing in platform 3. As we did so we were approached by the train conductor who advised us that there were three rowdy, drunken individuals in a compartment in one of the standard-class seating vehicles. They had refused to show him any tickets.

Wally was not the sort to let that go by as he was always a vigorous supporter of his staff. We entered the train and found the offending individuals. Wally identified himself and requested sight of their tickets. This request was met with abuse and an offer, by the oldest of the trio, to a fight out on the platform.

We left the train with a view to contacting a British Transport Police officer and were followed by the miscreant, who continued to shout abuse. As we stepped out of the train we noticed two very smart, tall individuals ambling along the platform. They were in military uniform, which suggested to us that they may have been military policemen. One had a self-rolled cigarette hanging from his lower lip and this soldier spoke to Wally, who, with his uniform and bowler hat, was clearly a railway official. 'Trouble guvnor?' he asked, while the miscreant continued to shout and threaten in the background, having been joined on the platform by his two colleagues, who were not so vocal.

Wally replied that the individuals did not appear to have tickets and that the man making most noise had threatened him with violence. Without further ado, one of the soldiers positioned himself behind the main offender and lifted him a few inches off the ground by his coat collar while, simultaneously, the second one lifted his knee up to connect with the man's groin. This caused the offender to bend his knees and, as he did so, he was dropped to the ground, ending up in a kneeling position.

The soldier with the cigarette then said, 'Maybe it would be a good idea to buy a ticket and not be so rude to this railwayman?' No further words were spoken as Wally and I looked on incredulously at the outcome of a sudden sequence of uninvited and unexpected actions which had taken no longer than thirty seconds from start to finish. The two soldiers continued their amble along the platform and joined the train. We had no idea what they were doing at Paddington or what their business was, since very few words were spoken.

The offending individuals were last seen making their way towards the booking office. The train left shortly thereafter. They missed it! Neither Wally nor I mentioned or reported this event to anyone else, choosing to regard it as 'rough justice', uninvited by us, but welcome nevertheless!

A POOR INVESTMENT

David Ward describes the catalogue of problems encountered with a new sleeping car design, including users falling out of bed

When I went to Euston in 1969 as regional passenger marketing manager, LMR, I became familiar with the operation of sleeping cars. At that time sleeping car services operated from Euston to Manchester, Liverpool, Holyhead, Preston, Barrow, Carlisle, Ayr/Stranraer, Glasgow, Perth and Inverness. To the provincial destinations, LMS-designed cars were used and to Carlisle and beyond Mark I sleepers were allocated, and I used these services regularly to attend meetings away from Euston. They enabled meetings to start at 8.30/9 a.m., finish before lunch, then have lunch on the train on the return journey and, on the shorter journeys, even permitted an hour back in the Euston office before going home. The cars were well designed for their time and the low overnight speeds generally provided a comfortable night's rest, particularly where arrival at destination was in the early hours of the morning and the cars were parked in a quiet platform until alighting time at about 8 a.m.

The life of these sleeping cars was, however, brought to an end by a serious fire in 1978 in a Mark I car at Taunton, caused by laundry stacked against an electric heater catching light and with fatalities and injuries due to smoke and the difficulty of exiting the vehicles. The design of the Mark III sleeping car, which had been in development for some time, was therefore brought forward and, based on the success of the Mark III day coach, its arrival was eagerly anticipated. However, it proved to be a great disappointment.

This was because the cost of building the new cars considerably exceeded the authorised expenditure and the number ordered had to be reduced to keep within spending limits. However, too many had been ordered in the first place and even the reduced number exceeded the number required for the services then operating, and twenty-eight surplus cars were leased to Denmark for several years. When they returned they were stored and then scrapped.

One of the BREL Derby-built Mark III sleeping cars intended for the nightly London–Aberdeen service. (David Ward)

Even allowing for the speed at which the cars were designed and built, it is hard to understand how the detail of the design had so many shortcomings. One reason was that a prototype had not been operated for a year to show up the faults before the production build was started; this undoubtedly played its part in the subsequent problems, but it is still hard to explain how so many obvious faults appeared in the final design.

The biggest problem was the bed. It had originally been intended that foam mattresses would be used and therefore a hard wooden base was specified. The Taunton fire, however, changed the specification of the mattress to 'interior sprung', but the bases were not changed to match this different kind of mattress, which resulted in a very hard bed. This was exacerbated by all the mattresses being only 2ft 3in wide, whereas in the Mark I sleeper the first-class mattress was 2ft 6in wide and the second-class mattress was 2ft 4in in width. One senior railway officer described it as 'like trying to sleep on top of a narrow wall'. Considerable thought was given to alleviating these problems, but eventually it was necessary to go to the very considerable expense of renewing all the 2,800 mattresses with a design that had a softer middle. This, however, did not solve the lack of width problem, and this narrowness could not be corrected because the width at the head-end was constrained by a bulkhead and at the foot-end by the washbasin stand.

The new mattresses were made to the same width of 2ft 3in because it was intended to make it possible to quickly convert the cabins from single (first class) to double (second class) berth, and the design provided for the top berth to be folded back into a pocket in the bulkhead wall. However, this pocket was not designed to be deep enough to incorporate the top mattress, so a problem arose over what to do with the mattress from the top berth.

The first solution was to put two mattresses on the bottom berth, with a claim that the doubling up provided more comfort for the first-class ticket holder. Unfortunately this arrangement proved unstable and resulted in passengers rolling out of bed! It also resulted in the tea shelf being upset if passengers raised their knees. The next solution was to carry the spare mattresses in a specified section of the guard's brake van. This proved unsatisfactory because the mattresses became damp and dirty as a result. Another alternative was

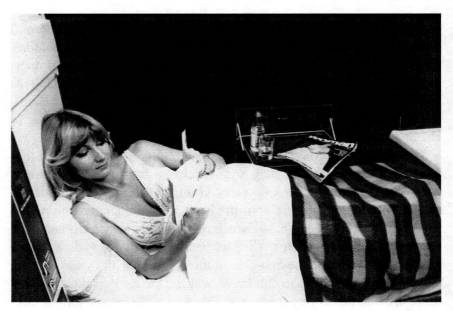

Publicity photograph of the interior of a berth in a Mark III sleeping car. (David Ward)

to place one berth in a car out of use, so it could be used for the storage of the surplus mattresses, but this was costly in lost revenue, because trains often ran with full payloads. Eventually convertibility was largely abandoned except between summer and winter seasons, when a change would be made to balance the difference in demand between first and second class for the whole season, with the surplus mattresses being stored at the home depot of the cars.

The plumbing proved to be another case of almost unbelievably bad design. The electric boiler and the pump pressure proved too weak to supply the berth hot-water taps if more than two or three were operated at once, which often happened at the critical time first thing in the morning, when passengers were getting up. Worse still, to drain an out-of-use vehicle of potentially freezable water during frosty weather, involved opening more than twenty drain cocks, some of which were not easily accessible. Even then it did not drain the vehicle completely because some of the pipework was horizontal, and therefore couldn't drain by gravity. At Bounds Green depot it was the practice to take a vehicle that was being drained up on to the approach gradient to the flyover and give it a few rough shunts to shake out all the water!

The fire alarm system also proved extremely sensitive, no doubt due to the lessons learned from the Taunton fire, and it could be set off by passengers using talcum powder or hair spray, thus causing unnecessary disturbance. It could also be triggered by fumes from diesel locomotives when the train was passing through tunnels.

The Mark I and ex-LMS sleeping cars had a 'potty' in the cabinet under the washbasin. In the Mark Is this was flushed by the 'grey' water when the wash basin was emptied, and this proved quite effective. The 'potty', however, was excluded from the Mark III sleeper for hygiene reasons and this resulted in misuse of the washbasins because some passengers were reluctant to walk to the toilets, which were at the end of the car, in the middle of the night. A procedure for regularly disinfecting the washbasins and their pipework had to be introduced and strictly enforced.

Finally: the air conditioning. The Mark III cars were totally enclosed from the outside except for the droplights or the four doors at the end of the vehicles. Therefore, if the air conditioning failed or could not be kept at an acceptable temperature, the only way of ventilating the berths was to prop the doors partially open with a pillow and rely on the air passing down the corridor from the end door open droplights. This was in marked contrast to the Mark I cars which were pressure-ventilated, but also had both the conventional drawlight and opening droplights in the doors.

Unfortunately, the air conditioning in the Mark III sleepers proved quite unreliable. The temperature in the berth could, in theory, be controlled by the passenger by a sliding switch that moved in a segment from hot to cold. The mechanism, however, was prone to failure and until it was repaired the temperature remained in the last position before failure. Furthermore, the motor alternator sets under the vehicles tended to be noisy and this could easily disturb passengers' sleep when these devices cut in and out as an electric locomotive passed through a neutral section. If the alternator set fuse blew then this could only be renewed at a depot and, as a result, all power was lost in the vehicle and the lights gradually drained the battery until they went out. The whole system was dependent upon the ETH supply from the locomotive and, if this or the engine failed, then so did the air conditioning, and the lights, again, gradually flattened the battery. The whole system was, therefore, far from being the 100 per cent reliable, a requirement that was essential for a sleeping car.

There were also other less serious irritations. The berth blinds had only two positions: fully open or fully closed. It was thus not possible to enjoy the outside view without the berth occupant being fully exposed. The Mark Is had a sliding shutter which could be fixed in any position. The retention toilets at the end of the new cars showed 'out or order' if the retention tanks were more than seven-eighths full. If the tanks had not been emptied at the last turnround, this resulted in passengers having to walk through the train to find a toilet which could be used.

In view of all the foregoing problems it might be asked whether these Mark III cars had any good points. The coach bodies certainly looked attractive and the air-sprung bogies rode quietly and well. The body and floor insulation against exterior and track noise was also excellent. In fact, it was almost too good because noise created within the coach could not escape and the sound of passengers walking or talking in the corridors could be intrusive.

All told, the Mark III sleepers were a costly and disappointing investment. It is, perhaps, a happy eventuality that the once-popular use of sleeper travel has been overtaken by day services being accelerated and starting much earlier and finishing much later, thus avoiding overnight journeys except for the longest distances.

WHAT'S IN A NICKNAME?

Small stations were like small communities. Bill Robinson recalls the one at Beverley where nicknames were the norm

Beverley is a small market town built amongst flat farmland on the edge of the Yorkshire Wolds. The arrival of the railway cut the town in half, necessitating many level crossings and signal boxes. My father, Bill Robinson (Senior), spent the early 1950s as signalman at Beverley Station Box. In those days the only communication with signal boxes was a circuit telephone which linked the local area. In the evening, when services were few and far between, signalmen would pass the time of day on the circuit talking about the events of the day.

Each signalman had a nickname. Bill Vickers was 'The Vicar', Stan Dean 'The Rural Dean' for his church attendance and Jack Dean was 'The Red Dean' because of his left-wing views. Percy O'Connel was 'Percy Fender', after a music hall artiste and Alan Barber became 'Ali BaBa'. Finally Gerry Alison, the relief signalman, was 'Dead Legs', the reason for which was to become apparent to me some time later.

As a junior clerk I was sent to Arram, the next station on the line, to carry out a passenger user census. It was February – a classic time to count passengers! I was to work the early shift, travelling on the first train and arriving just before 6 a.m. On my first day I stepped off the train to find that, apart from a couple of oil lamps on the platform and one in the box, the place was in darkness. For a few days I counted the passengers or their absence and observed the unchanging pattern of life at a country station. On the fourth morning I arrived to find the station in complete darkness and stumbled towards the signal box. On opening the door all was dark there too, but slowly I became aware of a figure laid out on a bench.

'Bill lad, just thoo pull number two lever and swing them gates,' came a voice from the gloom. It was Gerry Alison, the relief signalman. He never moved until almost 9 a.m., giving me instructions on working the box and also on selling tickets from the booking office. Now I realised why his nickname was 'Dead Legs', as he stayed horizontal for as long as possible every day! My dad's nickname was 'Dead Bod', the reason for which I never dared ask!

'THE YORKIE'S IN THE CUPBOARD'

This phrase from Basil Tellwright had Geoff Body digging out examples of the railway language he had collected over the years

Within his first few minutes in the yard inspector's office at Stanground Yard at Peterborough the first telephone message a young Basil Tellwright took consisted of the simple phrase, 'The Yorkie's in the cupboard'. It was soon followed by another announcing, 'The Derby's in the cupboard'. They were notifications from the signalman at Whittlesey Station North that a goods train destined for the ex-Great Northern New England Yard and one for the ex-Midland line to Stamford and Leicester had been diverted on to the Up Goods line on their way to Peterborough. The origin of 'Yorkie' lay in the first title of the Great Northern route as the London & York Railway, and of 'Derby' in the fact that the Midland Railway had its headquarters there.

As in other major industries, the railways had a rich language of their own, built up by railwaymen over a long history and essential for all new employees to learn if they wanted to feel part of their industry, and also to understand some of the things going on. Phrases such as, 'The bobby says he's dyked the fish because the ukelele needs a blow up, and he's giving the Mark Lane the road', would seem like a foreign language to the uninitiated, but only meant that the signalman had given preference to a certain passenger train by diverting a fish train while its locomotive had a chance to restore full steam pressure.

Yorkie and Derby were not the only names for former systems. Swedie was the label for anything Great Eastern, Wessie for the London

& North Western, with other examples like Lanky for the Lancashire
& Yorkshire system, Caley for the Caledonian and so on. The Great
Western did not get labelled in this way. Indeed, it liked to think of
itself officially as 'The Royal Road' from the early association with
Queen Victoria cemented in a speech by the Prince of Wales during
the company's centenary celebrations. Its detractors had used the
expression 'The Great Way Round' until the original via Bristol line
to the West was supplemented by the direct route through Westbury.

Other lines got re-interpretations of their initials, making the
Manchester, Sheffield & Lincolnshire, predecessor of the Great
Central, 'Money Sunk & Lost' and the tortured Oxford, Worcester
& Wolverhampton Railway 'The Old Worse and Worse'. A certain
Irish black humour was also revealed by calling the Ulster Transport
Authority system 'Ulster's Terrible Affliction'.

Since locomotives epitomised railway activity they had an incredible
variety of pet names, some of the later ones originating from railway
enthusiasts. The American system of names to indicate wheel arrangements, e.g. 'Pacific' for a 4-6-2 locomotive, was widely used and other
informal names derived from the characteristics of a particular design.
'Gobblers', for example, consumed a lot of coal and the appearance of
a class of 2 30 Lancashire & Yorkshire bulbous saddle tanks led to them
being referred to as 'Fat Nannies'. The Western gas turbine locomotives
were 'Kerosene Castles'!

Some terms were absorbed into official communications and vice
versa. Reference to a 'raft' of wagons or a 'rake' of coaches was totally
normal. Since a code book used for the once-widespread railway telegraph network abbreviated phrases into single words to speed trans-
mission it was inevitable that these, too, should pass into common and
wider user. The code words 'Goose' and 'Gosling', relating to traffic
acceptance restrictions, were typical examples. 'Cape' meant cancel
and added the expression 'caped' to everyday usage. Wagon types had
codes so that any bogie bolster wagon inevitably became, simply, a
'Bobol' and a flat wagon for carrying containers a 'Conflat'. The civil
engineer gave his various wagon types the names of sea creatures and
these were even painted on their sides.

Posh and official train names such as The Flying Scotsman and
Atlantic Coast Express were less familiar in practice than ones like
'The Beer' for the Cambridge Buffet Express, the 'Owl' and 'Waker' for

the Up and Down Penzance sleepers and 'The Tinto' for a Caledonian Railway Peebles to Glasgow service. Local trains got local names, e.g. 'Stratford Jack' and 'The Marlow Donkey', and some even took the names of trainmen who worked them regularly, 'Dolly Gray' and 'Freddie Free' among these. The GWR actually adopted the informal names in common use for its regular freight services so that the 22.00 service carrying Huntley & Palmers biscuits away from its Reading factory was always called 'The Biscuits'. 'The Meat' was a Birkenhead freight service, 'The Pedlar' one from Birmingham and the 12.04 Paddington to Worcester was, unsurprisingly, 'The Sauce'.

Local lines and places featured strongly in the informal terminology, mostly with a touch of irony. That was certainly the case with the unlovely Somers Town Goods Depot in London which those working there mockingly referred to as the 'Tea Gardens'. The jumble of buildings beside King's Cross terminus was 'The African Jungle' and the train crew lodging house at Swindon 'The Barracks'. There were several 'Crab and Winkle' coastal branch lines and the roundabout route from Wroxham to Norwich via Aylsham was generally known as 'Round the World'.

Equipment and practices did not escape the attentions of those intent on making them seem more human and familiar. Signal arms were referred to as a 'peg' or 'board', a ground signal as a 'dod' or 'dolly', the rule book as 'The Bible' and the meal that was taken to work in so many cases as 'snap' or 'bait'. Soliciting tips was commonly referred to as 'weazeling'.

The informal railway language, less used nowadays of course, was highly colourful and not without value. Lying behind the words themselves were origins that were often of considerable interest and significance. Some originated well before the railway era, like 'bait' which was a term well used and understood in the days of horse transport when horses had to be fed, i.e. 'baited', during their working day. Other words were coined in the very practicalities of railway life like 'Death Chamber' which described the sparks in the machinery compartment of the Liverpool–Southport–Ormskirk electric trains of earlier years. Yet other terms, possibly the most endearing, derived from the inherent humour and good nature of railwaymen. Calling the rail mounted viaduct inspection unit a 'Gozunder' and the bowler-hatted Haslemere commuters 'The Flour Graders' come under this latter heading.

Railway modernisation and increasing streamlining and sophistication has seen technical terms and sets of initial letters displace the older supplementary language. EMU and ATOC are fine, but do not have quite the same charisma as 'the old tongue'.

TRAINFERRY DILEMMA

David Jagoe describes the complications of a major and imaginative change in the trainferry service to Europe

BR's trainferry service was operated with five old, slow, limited-capacity vessels. Three were single rail-decked ships owned and operated by the French railways (SNCF) and sailing between Dover and Dunkerque. The other two were Sealink vessels sailing between Harwich and Zeebrugge, one of which had two short rail decks, with an unreliable lift to raise wagons on to the upper deck. While the vessels on the shorter Dover–Dunkerque route were each capable of making a round trip in twenty-four hours, those operating over the longer Harwich–Zeebrugge distance could only make a one-way trip in that time. The terminals, each with rail linkspans, were owned and operated by the Dover Harbour Board, ALA in Dunkerque, Sealink in Harwich and Ferry-Boats in Zeebrugge.

There was a long-standing convention in which income from each of the rail authorities involved, based on an agreed competitive market rate for each journey, was shared according to a distance-based formula. BR was at a great disadvantage due to the relatively short distances of the UK rail journeys and by the resultant meagre contributions towards the high costs of the shipping services. Despite several attempts to secure an improvement in the net position, BR was still 'bleeding' around £19 million a year due mainly to the over-resourcing. A new and radical approach was required.

Coinciding with a change of management in 1984, a new strategy was developed, principally with Armanant Naval (SNCF's equivalent of Sealink) and shared with our Sealink. This was based on the shorter Dover–Dunkerque sea route and on using a single larger and faster vessel with a complement of three crews, instead of the five smaller ships with their fifteen crews. The terminals would be reduced to two.

Many obstacles had to be overcome before this could happen, including pressure from sections of senior BR management for the retention of the traditional wagon load business and from the continental authorities who relied heavily on it. There were political pressures associated with the proposed introduction of the Channel Tunnel on a ten-year timeline, redundancy issues affecting both ports and vessels and the attitude of the German DB which saw loss of revenue on its northern traffic as a French–British conspiracy. Sealink wanted a larger role despite having no investment in the project.

Staff consultation meetings resolved the redundancy issues through redeployment opportunities in the port areas and the German reservations appeared to dissolve when the Ramsgate harbour owners offered to develop a linkspan facility to create a service to Ostend and Dunkerque. Objections to this arose from some residents who, together with the Dover Harbour Board, referred the matter to the Home Secretary. Finally, all these complicated issues were resolved and the development was focussed on Dover.

The new Trainferry vessel, to be known as *Nord Pas de Calais*, was built in Dunkerque and came into service in April 1988. She was rated with a speed of 22.5 knots which allowed a sailing time between Dover and Dunkerque of two hours. Designed with forward and stern access, the vessel had two decks, the lower with 600m of rail track in two lengths, of which 50m were uncovered and capable of being separated by dropping a bulkhead to permit the conveyance of dangerous and toxic cargo. The upper deck could accommodate forty heavy road vehicles, anathema to some in senior BR circles, but offering a welcome contribution to the cost of operation.

The single-track linkspans at Dover Western Dock and at Dunkerque were replaced by heavier and double-track versions. This permitted simultaneous and even loading, avoiding the vessel being tilted and, at the same time, ensuring a rapid turnround. The combination of a two-hour sailing time and a one-hour turnround in the ports enabled the vessel to make four round trips in twenty-four hours.

For vessel and port facilities the total capital outlay amounted to 300 million French francs, Armanant Naval meeting the investment costs at both ports to simplify payment arrangements. The BRB investment in terminals amounted to £100,000 for the realignment of track at Dover Western Docks. With the Channel Tunnel scheduled

Although designed and built for an intensive service, the graceful lines of *Nord Pas de Calais* are still very apparent. (David Jagoe)

to come into operation in 1988, the investment life of the project had to be limited to ten years. The BRB was eventually persuaded to 'buy forward' French francs at a very favourable rate of two to the pound and this reduced the true capital cost for the vessel to £150 million. Based on historical costs, calculating the return on investment and operating costs showed a surplus for the Railfreight International Business of £1 million in the first full year of operation, a financial turnround improvement of some £20 million.

On the traffic side, the vastly improved service and greatly increased capacity opened up opportunities to exploit the potential trainload market. Among the flows secured were a weekly train of car components and spares from Germany, cold rolled steel coil and sheet from Germany and France to Halewood and Dagenham, domestic 'white goods' from Italy, oranges, onions and tomatoes in season from Spain, newsprint from Scandinavia and, somewhat akin to 'coals from Newcastle', feta cheese from Scotland to Greece and Turkey. An exciting prospect that was vigorously pursued was that of a daily 1,000-tonne trainload of milk from the Cotswolds to a rail-connected creamery in Turin. Whilst the transit time and the service capacity 'ticked all the boxes', the potential of this movement was not realised as grass-fed cows produce a milk which, due to the high level of carotin, was too yellow for the white cheeses preferred by the Italian consumer. Regrettably, the contract went to Germany.

Just when all seemed to be going well, disaster struck during the second year of operation when the linkspan at Dover collapsed into the harbour, creating a relatively short, but nevertheless embarrassing, hiatus in the service. A few voices cried, 'I told you so', especially as there had been contrary opinions about the choice of contractor to build the structure. Furthermore, due to vigorous political pressure and the advanced construction and commissioning of the Channel Tunnel in December 1995, the Trainferry service was terminated three years earlier than planned. Had the service survived the planned project life it would have met all the investment criteria and proved a very inexpensive and profitable ongoing operating activity.

BOOKING CLERK AT HISTON

Derek Clark remembers with affection his time at a small Cambridgeshire station

In spite of the ominous presence of Dr Beeching at the helm of British Railways in the 1960s, one of the joys of working at a small station was the feeling of belonging to a team who displayed loyalty and respect combined with a wonderful sense of humour. In my own case, I thoroughly enjoyed my time at Histon, issuing tickets and dealing with the passengers on a daily basis. Our team comprised two booking clerks, two porters, a goods clerk, two foremen, a signalman and, of course, the stationmaster, who expected the best from his staff and was a whale on punctuality. If a train was due to leave at 10 a.m. then it left at 10 a.m. and not at 10.01 a.m. He was also a keen gardener and so it came as no surprise to us that on several occasions our station won first prize in the Station Gardens Competition.

Early turn for the booking clerk began at 7.30 a.m. with the onslaught of hordes of Chivers–Hartley staff arriving on the DMU (diesel multiple unit) train from St Ives (Cambs). There was only one minute for about twenty passengers to alight and for the station staff to get the train away on time at 07.42. One of the difficulties was collecting the tickets, as it was cheaper for regular passengers to buy a day return than to have a season ticket. The outward halves of the Edmondson tickets had to be collected in the space of one minute. The only way to do this in such a short time was to take out one of the 'bowls' in the till and use it like a collection plate in which the passengers could place their tickets.

After the 07.42 had left for Cambridge, there was enough time before the next train to go over to the porters' hut for a chat and a brew of the best tea on British Railways.

Some of the passengers were really delightful. One of our regulars on the 08.19 to Peterborough was a car salesman who, armed with licence plates, regularly bought a single ticket to Birmingham to pick up a new car there and drive it back to Histon. His greeting, 'Top of the morning to you', warmed the heart and, together with the excellent tea, set the tone for the rest of the day.

When I first arrived at Histon, one of my greatest joys was exploring the tickets in the rack and other miscellanea in the office. We had several LNER issues and a vast number of luggage labels, including vintage GER and GN&GE Joint examples. However, the supreme example of past railways was the GER seal, which was used on the leather bags containing the previous day's takings. These were then despatched by the 12.05 train to Cambridge. Seeing GER embossed in the wax felt as if I were being catapulted back in time.

A privilege of being a member of the station staff at Histon was access to the Chivers-Hartley canteen, where those taking lunch were offered desserts that were being 'tested' on both Chivers and BR staff before the products were put on the market. One of these culinary delights was lemon cheese, which was truly delicious, and it also kept me going for the rest of the day, which says a lot for Chivers-Hartley's products!

Two of the big customers who regularly made use of our parcels and goods services were Cavenders Canoes and Histon Farms. About every two weeks Cavenders would bring two or three canoes to the station, which were then conveyed by passenger train as parcels traffic. The canoes always went on the 16.16 to Cambridge, where they were subsequently transferred to various destinations. On one occasion three canoes arrived only fifteen minutes before the booked departure of the train. At best there was only just sufficient time to do the necessary paperwork and load the canoes into the parcels van. Mindful of the principle of 'punctuality without question at all times', there was feverish activity on my part to get the three canoes into the van without causing delay. With the assistance of one of the porters it could usually be done – just. Unfortunately, this time one of the canoes got stuck and would not budge an inch. We had to enlist the help of the stationmaster and the guard and somehow finally managed to 'shoehorn' the canoe in. Needless to say, the train, having arrived on time, was five minutes late leaving Histon! The stationmaster did not utter a word, but there was a glint in his eye that said, 'Don't you ever let anything like this happen again!'

A very dramatic incident was the affair with the runaway pig. Histon Farms often sent livestock up to Scotland, usually pigs, and these were normally conveyed in a horsebox. Strictly speaking, the procedure for loading was the responsibility of both the goods clerk and the foreman, but on this particular occasion all the station staff were involved. Usually the animal could be loaded without any difficulty at all. This time, however, the pig rebelled. It refused to enter the horsebox and no amount of coaxing or cajoling would induce the creature to budge from the goods yard. We pushed and pulled, but to no avail. Then, all of a sudden, the pig broke loose, ran round the yard and then on to the Up platform, careering up and down, squealing like mad. To add to the confusion, there were shrieks from a potential lady passenger, who had been patiently waiting to buy a ticket to Wisbech. With everyone chasing the pig backwards and forwards there was a period of complete chaos until the foreman, bless his heart, finally managed to seize the errant creature close to the goods yard, giving sufficient time for the rest of us to push it into the horsebox. At that point, the pig capitulated and decided that it had lost the battle and thereupon became reasonably docile and actually seemed quite willing to undergo its long trip up to Scotland.

For me Histon was an enjoyable 'grass roots' experience never to be repeated in subsequent promotions. I have never forgotten what the Histon stationmaster said to me both at the beginning and at the end of my time there, viz, 'On the railways there are two things you must have: a sense of humour and a commitment to absolute punctuality.'

FORGOTTEN COLLAR

Philip Benham learned a lesson during a spell in charge of single-line working in the middle of the night in darkest Rutland

Extra safeguards are needed where trains run over the same line in opposite directions, because of the exceptional risks of a head-on collision. On single-line routes these safeguards are built into the signalling, the traditional method being a train staff or token which has to be carried by each driver. As there is only one staff provided, or one token released by the signalling system, two trains cannot enter a single line section at the same time.

But single-line working (SLW) can also be necessary on a double-track railway. If one line is blocked, perhaps by a derailment, or more commonly during engineering works, allowing trains to run in both directions on the other line keeps the job going. In this situation a pilotman is appointed to personally authorise the driver of every train on to the single line. So that he can easily be recognised, the pilotman wears a special armband or carries a red flag, and when the next train will be coming from the opposite end of the section, he rides through with the driver.

The rules for SLW were laid down in the railway Rule Book in every detail. For a newly appointed, and very green, inspector charged

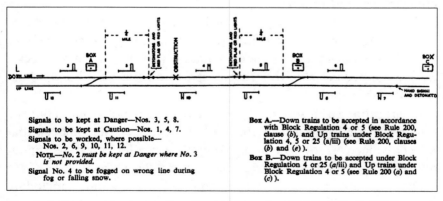

Signals to be kept at Danger—Nos. 3, 5, 8.
Signals to be kept at Caution—Nos. 1, 4, 7.
Signals to be worked, where possible—
   Nos. 2, 6, 9, 10, 11, 12.
NOTE.—*No. 2 must be kept at Danger where No. 3 is not provided.*
Signal No. 4 to be fogged on wrong line during fog or falling snow.

Box A.—Down trains to be accepted in accordance with Block Regulation 4 or 5 (see Rule 200, clause (*b*), and Up trains under Block Regulation 4, 5 or 25 (a/iii) (see Rule 200, clauses (*b*) and (*e*)).
Box B.—Down trains to be accepted under Block Regulation 4 or 25 (a/iii) and Up trains under Block Regulation 4 or 5 (see Rule 200 (*a*) and (*c*)).

The single-line working instruction diagram from the 1950 Rule Book. (Philip Benham)

with applying them for the first time during night-time engineering between Manton Junction and Luffenham in Rutland, they looked particularly daunting. SLW forms had to be filled out, the correct train register book entries made in each signal box, the signalmen told which signals to keep at danger, and hand-signalmen, provided by the permanent way department, briefed on their duties. Oh, and don't forget to ensure the catch points halfway through the section are clipped, scotched and locked – otherwise any train going in the wrong direction will be derailed (just as happened to a friend on another region a few weeks back!).

It was around 2 a.m. and all was going well. I had ridden through the section from Manton to Luffenham, and supervised the shunting of a train through the crossover at Luffenham to get on to the opposite line, before accompanying it through to Manton. Nor had I forgotten to display my armband to the staff working the tamping machine on the blocked line, so they knew in which direction to look for the next train to pass. A train was on its way from Oakham towards Manton Junction, but there was just time to grab my sandwiches from the car.

Manton Junction signal box is situated immediately south of Manton Tunnel, in the apex of the two lines diverging towards Corby and Stamford. As I walked back from the car, the Toton–Whitemoor coal train emerged from the tunnel, and I heard the throb of its Class 44 diesel accelerating away over the single line. It had not stopped, and I had most definitely not given authority for the train to enter this part of the track.

So what had gone wrong? I rushed up the box steps to remonstrate with the signalman. He was Chinese, and, although experienced, his English was not the best. The explanation was unclear, but it seems he saw no need to stop the train as it was on the right line and did not need shunting.

Clearly this was a serious breach of the rules, but what about my own responsibility? The one thing I had forgotten was to check that a lever collar was in place on the signal levers that had to be kept at danger as a reminder to the signalman not to clear them.

Over the next few years I was to apply SLW many times, including in emergencies when there was no chance to pre-plan, but I never forgot about lever collars. And what were the consequences of this particular misdemeanour? Well it was two o'clock in the morning, and Manton Junction was very remote!

UNDER THE BOWLER HAT

The district inspectors were key figures in railway operating safety and efficiency, as Bill Parker makes clear

A bowler hat was traditional wear for district inspectors (DIs). They were not part of the free official uniform issue, but had to be paid for by each individual, so not every DI wore one! My stationmaster father was so pleased with my appointment as DI that he treated me to a bowler from Dunn's in the Liverpool Street Arcade, but it did cause some ribaldry from my family and non-railway friends when I tried it on at home.

Another DI peculiarity was membership of 'The Cloth'. I became aware of this odd title when I became general assistant to the Cambridge divisional traffic manager and was greeted by Chief District Inspector Cyril Rose with an earthy welcome to 'The Cloth', and the aside, 'I suppose you'll do'! This was despite the fact that I was a relative youngster in my mid-twenties, never a signalman but now in charge of the inspectorate. DTM Alan Suddaby told me many years later that his reasoning had been, 'If you can't beat 'em, get someone to join 'em.'

The DIs of old were generally regarded as very prestigious and supe-rior people, typified by the Peterborough DI, whom I met during early unofficial visits as a youngster with my father to signal boxes. He was a portly man with a florid face, bulging out of his overcoat and, topped by his bowler, he looked rather like a black snowman. Despite this, whenever I was 'caught' he always explained to me what was happen-ing, prefaced with, 'Now listen lad, and watch!'

District inspectors were the eyes and ears of, and reported directly to, the senior operating officers and had exceptional powers over all operating department staff. Their experience and competence ena-bled them to put their hands to virtually any operating task, ranging from ensuring staff competence to taking charge of line emergen-cies. Both respected and feared, they were generally 'wired on' via the internal telegraph system and in some areas they had their own totally irregular unofficial bell code and nicknames. My nickname was 'Call Attention', coined because the strict application of that bell signal was one of my earlier initiatives; other DIs fared far worse than that!

In one bi-annual re-examination I was obliged to fail a long-standing stationmaster in his knowledge of rules and regulations. He complained strongly about that 'young lad having the effrontery of treating a widely experienced railwaymen in such a way'. The chief inspector failed him too, with serious consequences, but at least the event did nothing to harm my standing and, thanks to the grapevine, other staff quickly became 'genned-up' for their future examinations!

A most enjoyable task came when I was involved with the combining of Stamford East (ER) and Stamford Junction (LMR) signal boxes. I learned later that there had been a bit of friendly betting between the ER and LMR senior signal engineers about whether a DI would be capable of producing a signalling plan for such a project. Knowing the others involved quite well, and having time on my hands because my new wife was sadly having a long stay in hospital, I was able to devote a lot of time to this task. I spent hours drawing the new layout of the location and detailing the signals required, the track-circuiting, the changed levers for signals, points and lockbars, their numbering in the signal box, the bells and block instruments, the single line electric token apparatus for the Essendine branch and the interlocking diagram, and even the telegraph communication equipment!

The LMR signal engineer's people lost their friendly bet and my 'reward' was an invitation to a very pleasant regional Signal Sighting Committee visit luncheon. The only complaint raised was by the East Box signalmen that they would lose the opportunity to fish in the River Welland from the ledge at the top of their signal box steps!

NIGHTS ON THE TAY BRIDGE

Two nights, spent high above the River Tay on Europe's longest railway bridge, remain vivid for Jim Dorward

Sunday 28 June 1959

It is shortly after midnight and I am on the Tay Bridge on the East Coast Main Line at Dundee. This is Europe's longest railway bridge. I am with a colleague from the Perth District Engineer's office and, most importantly, engineers from BRHQ.

Possession of the Down and Up lines has been taken for tests to measure the stress in the main girders when carrying trains, now that the expansion bearing renewal programme is almost complete. As the old bearings were seized up, they prevented the girders from expanding and contracting freely, thereby creating unwelcome additional stresses.

Two 4-6-2 Pacific steam locomotives have been ordered for a series of 'passes' over one of the spans that have the new expansion bearings. Fereday-Palmer stress recorders have been attached to the girders at the high stress points. I am keen to discover which engines have been allocated to the task, as I have seen all the likely contenders many times on Edinburgh–Aberdeen trains. When they arrive on the bridge, I am disappointed and the HQ engineers annoyed, as the combined efforts of Dundee and Edinburgh Haymarket sheds only provides two 2-6-2 Class V2 locomotives.

However, the tests are carried out before daylight and the results seem to confirm expectations – the new bearings are working.

Sunday 19 July 1959

It is about two o'clock in the morning and I am on the Tay Bridge again. This time, I am on the bridge to see how the new expansion bearings are actually installed. This is indeed heavy engineering, as one end of the span in question has to be jacked up a few inches to provide enough clearance for the old bearings to be moved out and the new ones slid in.

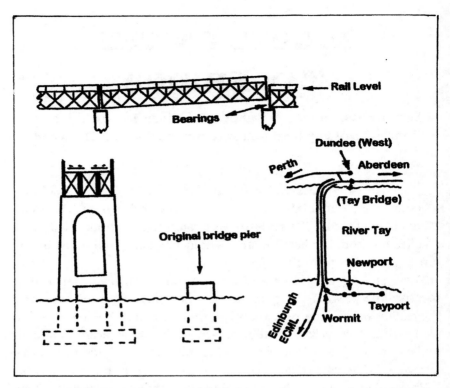

A diagram of the Tay Bridge lines and the bearing replacement work carried out. (Jim Dorward)

The outer main girders of each span (not *the* 'High Girders') were, surprisingly, used in the original bridge, part of which fell, along with a train, into the river in the infamous disaster of 28 December 1879, claiming the lives of the seventy-five passengers and crew.

I am with the engineer from the Chief Civil Engineer's Bridge Section in Glasgow, who is in charge of the operation. It has been taking place on Sundays for several months, with trains diverted via Perth. We climb down inside the space that has just been created above the pier, to see the work at close quarters. By now, the men involved have developed a very efficient procedure so that, to the onlooker, it all looks quite straightforward.

As I discovered a few days ago that Bertram Mills Circus is moving overnight from Perth to Arbroath, I make a point of seeing one of their four special trains passing along the Perth–Dundee line, at 25mph, where it runs parallel with the Tay Bridge at Magdalen Green. The train was on time and had about ten bogie flat wagons conveying about twenty circus road vehicles.

I have now walked back to the span where the work is being carried out. Now comes the tricky bit! The bridge engineer, who is used to climbing all over the bridge, says that he should show me one of the new bearings with a main girder actually sitting on it. So we walk along the track to a suitable span. To my horror he says, 'Right, we go over the parapet here and climb down the outside temporary ladder.'

HAPPY FAMILIES 1992

Terry Worrall's introduction of Her Majesty the Queen to the staff at the Wolverton Works produced an unexpected rejoinder

During my time at the British Railways Board HQ as passenger operations manager from 1983, one of my tasks was to take charge of the Royal Train rebuild project which involved both new vehicles and the refurbishment of some existing ones. Design work was carried out by the director of mechanical & electrical engineering (DM & EE) team at Derby and construction by the then British Rail Engineering Ltd (BREL) team at Wolverton. This most interesting project involved many different staff, but the main workload was borne by the Wolverton team, initially under the direction of the works manager, Tony Roche, and later Andrew Gaskin.

This project took eight years to complete, with the Royal Train ending up comprising fourteen vehicles. During this time I had occupied three different posts at the Board and at the completion of the project I was Director of Operations, but I had retained responsibility for the project for the sake of continuity and for security reasons.

Prior to completion, I approached Sir Robert Fellowes (now Lord Fellowes), Her Majesty the Queen's Private Secretary, to see whether the Queen would agree to meet those members of the Wolverton team who had been working tirelessly in the background for eight years, as a way of recognising their commitment, professionalism and high-quality workmanship. This was agreed, and the team assembled, together with myself, at Liverpool Lime Street station immediately after an occasion when the Queen had visited the city. The Queen would take a few minutes to meet the staff prior to boarding her train.

The team was lined up alongside the train and I was to introduce its members by name and give a brief outline of the work undertaken by each individual. I needed to remember all the details; there could be no mistakes.

The event proceeded according to plan and, when I came to the end of the line, I introduced the last individual, my words being: 'Ma'am this is Mr Tapp, the plumber.' To the amusement of those within earshot the Queen responded immediately by saying, 'This is just like Happy Families!'

(Note: Happy Families is a card game, very popular many years ago, which features characters with names relating to their occupation – as it happens the 'plumber' in the official card game is referred to as 'Mr Pipe'!)

FROM JUNIOR TYPIST TO CHAIRMAN'S PA VIA LAND'S END AND JOHN O'GROATS

Railway management owed much to and asked much of its secretariat, as Margaret Ritchie's account reveals

My forty-eight-year railway career started in 1960 when my Uncle Willie prompted my appointment to a junior typist vacancy in the Chief Accountant's office, Glasgow, where he also worked. I was 15 years of age. The seven typists occupied two rooms which were heated by coal fires. Furniture was basic, typewriters manual and the hours 8.30 a.m. to 5 p.m. Monday to Friday with an hour for lunch. My

Chairman's PA Margaret Ritchie at her desk. (Margaret Ritchie)

pay was £3 4s 2d per week from which I gave £2 to my mother. It was a happy office where we had lots of fun. Practical jokes included removing parts from typewriters and hiding them, we had a party at Halloween and we each put 2s 6d into a kitty each week and when sufficient funds had accumulated we all went out together for evening dinner. It was my job to make the tea each morning and afternoon and the open fire was useful for heating pies, etc. Lena Smith, the supervisor, kept a friendly discipline over us and forty years later I still met three of my colleagues from this era for an annual get-together.

I had started on the bottom rung as a Grade A typist. Training on the job was then the order of the day. Lena made sure I increased my typing and shorthand speeds and I was upgraded to Grade B. In 1964 the Chief Accountant's office merged into the General Manager's office, where I became a typist in a larger typing pool. We now had electric typewriters and I was sent out occasionally as a relief secretary.

When the new Scottish Region HQ at Buchanan House was opened we all moved there where there were separate audio and copy-typing pools. I was placed in the audio pool and graded as a supervisor over a group of other typists. The audio arrangement was known as the

Assman system. Writers requiring their letters typed telephoned a number which connected them to a disc on to which they dictated their letter. The discs were allocated to typists to share out the workload evenly. They then typed the letter by playing the disc through headphones, with play being controlled by a foot pedal. The quality of dictation varied so much work had to be retyped, and the hitherto personal contact with the writer was lost. Typists' output was monitored and we were only allowed a twenty-minute break morning and afternoon. It was an unfeeling system and it was said of it 'what the writer did with his fingers the typist did with her foot'.

In 1974 I transferred to the General Manager's office, Euston, for personal reasons. Transfers could be made between regions, but only by reverting to the starting grade. I therefore took two steps back on the ladder, but quickly regained one step through appointment to a vacancy in the typing pool. Because few girls had shorthand ability I soon spent considerable time as a relief secretary, which gave me another grade. This in turn led to promotion to secretary to the Regional Passenger Marketing Manager, where my job branched out into interesting front-line railway work.

My first adventure was in 1977 when two ladies were required to dress in 1927 outfits as part of the promotion for the fiftieth anniversary of the *Royal Scot* train. We were sent to a theatrical costumiers in Camden and fitted out accordingly. For the anniversary run locomotive No. 87001 *Royal Scot* was used. At Euston we were required to stand at the front of the locomotive along with a retired Camden driver, Dick Allen, for press photographs. Dick was a great character, having spent a lifetime on the footplate. All three of us then travelled on the train to Glasgow where we were entertained at a Scottish dinner at the Central Hotel. Dick, who had an uncertain gait from a lifetime of steadying himself on the footplate, declared he was certain alcohol crystals had formed in his knee joints. As for me I soon found I had been bitten all over my upper body because the 1927 costume was infested with fleas!

My next assignment was at the memorial service for Bishop Eric Treacy at Appleby station. This was a major event, with two trains to convey the guests from London and the West Riding. Bishop Treacy had become known as 'The Railway Bishop' because of his pastoral interest in railway staff of all grades, and as the greatest railway photographer of his generation. Four thousand people attended

Arm-in-arm with retired driver Dick Allen, Margaret Ritchie poses in 1927 era costume before the *Royal Scot* Jubilee train sets out for Glasgow. (Margaret Ritchie)

the open-air service in the station goods yard with five bishops in attendance. My job was to look after Mrs Treacy and ensure she was briefed and in the right place for each item in the day's itinerary. Two weeks before the event I went to Mrs Treacy's home in Crosthwaite to agree the details with her. She and her sisters could not have been more charming. Six months later Class 86 locomotive No. 86240, which had hauled the London train between Euston and Farrington Junction, was named *Bishop Eric Treacy* at Penrith station and again I was deputed to look after Mrs Treacy, including when she was in the cab of the locomotive from Penrith to Carlisle.

Also in 1979, I was asked to model the new female uniform for staff who would be manning the Advance Passenger Train (APT). A uniform was made to fit me and I was sent over to BR HQ for the chairman to approve. He lifted my skirt to feel the quality of the cloth and thereafter that became a story to tell!

For the rest of my time at Euston I was often asked to look after guests or VIPs at ceremonies or on trains. In particular, I remember a special train to Mount Sorrell for the opening of the new Redland stone terminal on which Dr Beeching, later their chairman, was a passenger, and on a special train in 1982 from King's Cross to Edinburgh to launch the new Mark III sleeping cars, a vehicle and its shortcomings which I subsequently became very familiar with.

In 1982 the InterCity Sector was established at BR HQ Marylebone and Special Passenger Trains was separated into a separate sub sector with its own coaching stock, locomotives and catering staff. I transferred to this sector as customer services manager, which incorporated secretarial duties for the director special trains. Special trains business increased enormously, particularly at the first-class full dining end, and I found myself hosting or managing trains on a regular basis.

These VIP trains fell into two categories, viz. hospitality trains sold to businesses for the conveyance of their guests to functions or sporting events, and luxury trains run as part of the InterCity business for days out or longer three-day tours, entitled 'Land Cruises'. The former category, amongst many others, included trains for the Ford Motor Company to Northampton to launch their new 'Sierra' car and a similar train to Witham to launch their new 'Granada'. William Grant hired a special train including sleeping cars from King's Cross to Dufftown, where the station was adjacent to their Glenfiddich Distillery. Nothing could be left to chance with these trains and great attention was given to perfecting the detail, but occasionally we could be caught out, for example when the electric locomotive named *Glenfiddich* backed down on to a special train for Martell Brandy, which was taking their guests to the Grand National. We made certain such an embarrassment did not occur again.

The high profile of these trains can be judged from those run to York for the Sheriffs' Millennium and to Sandy for the RSPB (Royal Society for the Protection of Birds). The Sheriffs' Millennium train was required to convey all the great and the good from the law, including the Lord Chancellor and Lord Chief Justice, to York for a service at York Minster. HRH the Duke of York was the guest of honour and he also travelled on the train. The carriages were specially prepared at Bounds Green, providing 252 first-class dining seats. All the white roofs were repainted, the wheel tyres white-walled and the train cleaned to perfection. It looked a picture. However, three days before the train was due to run the operating manager became concerned at the consequences if it was delayed. The prized carriages were therefore hauled by two Class 90s with a standby Class 47 locomotive available at Peterborough. Apart from making certain everything was all right for HRH, my other memory of this train was when showing the chairman to his seat in a Mark I Open First-Class Saloon, Lady Reid commented to her husband, 'This is more comfortable than Mark IIIs.'

The RSPB train to Sandy was high profile because among the guests was the Prime Minister, Mrs Margaret Thatcher. The carriages had been prepared to perfection, but two incidents occurred which nearly created great embarrassment. Sir Robert Reid was on holiday, so Deputy Chairman David Kirby stood in for him at King's Cross to welcome the Prime Minister. On arrival he was not satisfied with the cleanliness of the platform. The mechanical sweeper was therefore summoned to give it another clean. Unfortunately, the hose connecting the brushes to the waste bin was perforated and the deputy chairman's new suit was showered with dirt! Then, at Bounds Green, it was found that the bolt securing the rear vestibule sliding door was out of alignment and could not be secured, so the empty train was late leaving the depot. Delay then occurred on the approach to King's Cross. Eventually an instruction was given that all other movements must cease to get the empty train into the platform. It arrived just as the Prime Minister was stepping out of her car in the parcels square. It was a close-run situation and the upshot was that instructions were issued that in future whenever Mrs Thatcher travelled by train it was to be run under the Royal Train regulations.

The InterCity Scenic Land Cruises and Luxury Days Out provided luxury travel to almost anywhere in the British Isles including Orkney, Iona, Skye, Isles of Scilly, Mull of Galloway, Cambrian Coast and Snowdonia. They ran summer and winter and the trains conveyed sleeping cars as well as day coaches. These excursions became very popular, but needed a lot of managing to keep them to their itinerary, particularly as off-train partners were involved and also the making arrangements for briefing the passengers, many of whom had not travelled on a train for years.

An illustration will suffice to indicate the type of problems which could occur. A cruise was organised to enable passengers to see the splendours of the West Highland and Kyle line all in one three-day tour. One train ran from Euston to Kyle and the other from King's Cross to Mallaig. Both had the same formations and passengers were to transfer from one train to the other via the Mallaig to Kyle of Lochalsh ferry, operated by MacBraynes. There is a well-known saying in Scotland that, 'The Earth is the Lord's and all that it contains, with the exception of the Western Isles and they belong to MacBraynes'. And so it proved on this tour.

I arrived on time with the Mallaig train. All passengers were told to be on the quay for the 12.00 sailing to Kyle. However, on arriving at the MacBrayne's office I found the Kyle ferry had been cancelled and the problem of moving the passengers to Kyle was mine. Mallaig has no bus depot and the train crew had returned to Fort William. We were stranded! However, the 11.30 ferry to Skye had not gone so, reluctantly, the MacBrayne's manager agreed to hold it until 11.45. This would give me enough time to round up the passengers and, hopefully, arrange through the BR traffic supervisor at Kyle for two coaches to be sent to Armadale to convey the passengers to the Kyle ferry. So far so good, but I arrived at the ferry gangway breathless with two passengers missing and the master of the ferry shouting down at me from his bridge that he was removing the gangway in a minute's time and me shouting back at him, asking for another five minutes. Fortunately the missing passengers appeared before the master carried out his threat and we all set sail for the forty-five-minute crossing to Armadale. I had left a message at Kyle regarding the need for the two coaches, but I did not know if my request could be met. Thankfully, when we arrived at Armadale the coaches were there and took us to Kyleakin, although even now I do not know if they were intended for us! We arrived in Kyle almost on time.

Overnight the Land Cruises would be parked up in a quiet scenic location so that passengers could join their sleeping berths when they pleased. The places used were Levisham, Ardgay, Spean Bridge, Towyn, Kyle of Lochalsh and Oban. Similarly, the train could sometimes be stopped in a scenic location for dinner to be served. Such places were alongside Loch Carron, Loch Etive and the Lindores Loch. My Scottish accent also usually opened the door for special favours such as a five-minute stop on Glenfinnan Viaduct.

As the operation of diesel multiple units on ordinary services expanded, the expertise for operating hauled trains declined, particularly in Scotland. It was, therefore, necessary for the train managers to be trained on key operational aspects. I went through a training

Train manager's reward for a taxing job; Margaret Ritchie enjoying hers on The Highlander. (Margaret Ritchie)

course at Bounds Green so that I became knowledgeable in the operation of the air brake, buckeye couplings and the fire alarm system on sleeping cars. The Class 37 locomotives used in Scotland were prone to overcharging the brake, with the result that when the locomotive was changed the brakes dragged. Showing guards how to release the brakes was therefore essential.

The director special trains was also responsible for the business arrangements for the Royal Train and when his manager dedicated to this work was on leave I deputised for him, acting as the liaison between the palace private secretaries, the Royal Train manager at Wolverton and the chief operating manager.

Chris Green presenting Margaret Ritchie with her InterCity Silver Swallow Excellence Award. (Margaret Ritchie)

In 1993 I was awarded the InterCity Silver Swallow Excellence Award as a commendation for my customer service activities, something I was very proud to receive.

Privatisation in 1994 brought most of these activities to an end and I decided to go back to my first love of secretarial work and became personal assistant to the managing director, north and west train-operating companies, based at Euston House. This was an interim organisation. The three business sectors were abolished, special trains sold off and the train-operating companies prepared for franchising by the franchising director. This work had its moments, but I missed being on the front line railway and, as the TOCs (train-operating companies) were franchised off, it was a declining occupation. Shortly before the end I was appointed to the position of personal assistant to the new franchising director, John O'Brien, at Goldings House, London Bridge. I therefore became a civil servant. Two years later franchising was absorbed into the Strategic Rail Authority (SRA). Mike Grant was appointed chief executive and I became his PA.

Sir Alistair Morton was chairman of the SRA and I occasionally did work for him. He was also chairman of the British Railways Board, a

The first new era steam-hauled train on the Settle & Carlisle line. Standing in front of No. 4771 *Green Arrow*, Margaret Ritchie presents a framed photograph of the locomotive to Bill Harvey, the man who restored her. (Margaret Ritchie)

position which still existed to deal with BR's residual assets and liabilities. He always had a twinkle in his eye and he put me back on a BR contract of employment. Richard Bowker succeeded Sir Alistair and he quickly established himself as chairman and chief executive and he appointed me as his PA. Despite the criticisms, the SRA did much good work, including the upgrade of the Southern power supply for the new electric multiple units and putting the West Coast Main Line modernisation on a sound business basis. When Richard Bowker left the SRA before its work was transferred to the Department of Transport he declared that in a few years' time it would be found necessary to set up a similar independent organisation to manage the railways. How right this prophesy has proved to be.

David Quarmby succeeded Richard Bowker as chairman of the SRA for its final year and I stayed on as his PA. As the work reduced I helped Dr Terry Gourvish, who had been commissioned to write the official history of the privatised railway, by searching out for him all the key official papers.

I retired in April 2006. David Quarmby arranged a magnificent retirement ceremony for me on the Bluebell Railway. He invited all my five previous bosses. I thought none of them would attend, but they all turned up. The event started with lunch at a hotel close to the Bluebell Railway, where many generous comments were made about me, some of which proved cleverly back-handed when John O'Brien asked my other bosses about my job interviews. They all agreed it was me who interviewed them! I was presented with a cased model of locomotive No. 47823 named SS *Great Britain* on one side and *Margaret Ritchie* on the other, together with a brass plaque commemorating the event and recording the names of my five previous bosses. After lunch we all went to the Bluebell Railway, where I was given a footplate ride on SR locomotive No. 1638, followed by afternoon tea in the railway's former GNR Directors' Saloon. It was a magnificent tribute and, I thought at that time, the end of my career.

However, two days later Richard Bowker telephoned me to say he had been appointed chief executive of the National Express Group and asked me if I would come out of retirement to be his PA. I was honoured to receive this request and I agreed to accept the offer for a two-year period. This was another experience in a different environment and brought my total service on the railways up to forty-eight years. Having finally retired, I then took on the job of Honorary Administrative Officer for the Settle & Carlisle Railway Trust, so I can claim I had a railway career exceeding fifty years.

RAIL TRAFFIC COPS

Checking drivers' speeds was a necessary job, but not one Philip Benham greatly enjoyed doing

As a divisional inspector at Nottingham, one of the less popular jobs was the carrying out of speed checks to ensure a driver was not exceeding the line or train speed limit. In power box areas, one way to measure train speed was to observe the time taken over a particular section of line, depicted by track circuit occupation on the signal box illuminated diagram. However, there was a flaw to this system, as the trade unions had successfully argued that the time of track occupation and diagram illumination might not precisely match. Thus to ensure fairness we had to an add an additional three seconds to the recorded measurements, which meant that only the most flagrant over-speeding cases were likely to be picked up.

A more reliable method was to record speeds from the lineside using a radar device. Unlike today, this was a bulky disc on a stand connected to a box with a display unit that read out the speed. A movements inspector and traction inspector worked together to ensure the recorded speed was verified. Sites such as major junctions were often chosen because of the need for trains to slow down through the junction. If an over-speed was registered, the controlling signal box was advised so arrangements could be made for the driver to be challenged. Anything other than a small infringement was likely to lead to him being formally disciplined.

As you can imagine, we were really popular with drivers when observed carrying out this task. Reactions ranged from a long blast on the horn (definitely more than the Rule Book requirements for 'staff on or about the line') through to some distinctly unfriendly gestures. Strangely enough, after the first couple of trains had passed, subsequent ones always knew we were there! The railway's grapevine rivalled today's electronic media in its speed and effectiveness.

What the drivers may not have known was that we inspectors did not much like the work either. It may have been a necessary monitoring process, but I felt uncomfortable trying to catch drivers out, although we always played fair by avoiding hiding behind bridge arches, as some were reputed to be doing. It was also very boring work and often extremely cold, standing around for hours on end with little action. I have some very mixed memories of cold winter afternoons around the junctions at Trent and Syston which were particularly exposed.

There is an amusing sequel. An inspector in another division – let's just call him Jack – was caught speeding by the police in his yellow railway van. By good fortune he had the railway radar equipment in the back, and the two PCs were so interested in this find that Jack was let off with a caution – a common bond perhaps.

WEST OF ENGLAND

The most rewarding time of Geoff Body's transport career was the period he spent in the West Country

From my first day as a temporary probationary junior male clerk at St Neots, LNER to leaving my post as director and general manager of Pickford Tank Haulage Ltd there was no more fruitful and happy period than the years I spent as marketing & sales manager of the Western Region's West of England Division at Bristol. Our territory was that beautiful part of Britain stretching from Worcester and the Lickey Bank in the north, to Swindon to the east and then all the way west to Penzance. The division had a first-class management team under the able and likeable Henry Sanderson, whose two assistants were genial Norfolk-born operator Clive Rowbury and Ken Painter, whose army tales included driving a main line locomotive on to the street tramway network in one of the Asian arena cities.

My opposite number was good friend Bill Bradshaw – later Lord Bradshaw – who controlled operating matters from an office in the impressive Jacobean-style headquarters building of the old Bristol & Exeter Railway, ably assisted by Alec Bath and Maurice Holmes. The region was well guided by general managers Ibbotson and then Bonham-Carter, and we were all tasked with lifting it out of a soporific introspection which lingered on from the glory days of the Great Western Railway. Going to work at this period had the added bonus of driving along Bristol's Portway, through the Avon Gorge and often with a vessel moving along the parallel river.

The large and varied area covered by the division was reflected in its traffics. Prestige passenger services operated on the main line via Swindon, on the West of England route via Westbury, to Worcester via Oxford and on the cross-country artery from the north via Birmingham. Bristol, Bath, Taunton, Exeter, Torbay and Plymouth were important traffic centres, each with its connections providing services for places like Yeovil, Barnstaple, Minehead and Newquay. The ex-Southern Railway main line to Exeter was still open, but was soon to be singled and other rationalisation was in the air, including the benefits of multi-aspect signalling at Bristol. Dozens of excursions,

A scene at the Port of Fowey with Cornish china clay which has been worked down from St Blazey being loaded to vessel.

Music fans from an early Glastonbury Festival crowd on to a train at Castle Cary.

charter trains and other specials were run and on summer Saturdays all senior staff were out and about to make sure things ran smoothly.

Bristol produced significant freight movements, including that of chocolate, tobacco and the imports through Avonmouth Docks, plus the business of the firms located on its estate, like Rio Tinto Zinc and the ICI. Coal came into the coal concentration centres at Filton and Wapping Wharf. Mendip stone graduated from small beginnings to a massive trainload operation, tinplate arrived in quantity for Metal Box at Worcester and there was a lot of scrap moving about. The Far West, as it was known, yielded huge tonnages of china clay and ball clay as well as a very busy broccoli season, which followed on from the boat-loads of daffodils brought into Penzance from the Scilly Islands. Milk in tanks was despatched from creameries at Bason Bridge, Totnes and Torrington, and the North Somerset coalfield was still lowering some of its output down the siding inclines to Radstock Yard.

Life got a bit hectic on occasions. A continuous downpour around Bristol shortly after my arrival had us all in the control office for hours, trying to rescue people from trapped trains and then clearing the lines and restoring services. Another deluge, a more human one, attended the rather unexpected popularity of the first Glastonbury Festival. A bad accident at Ashchurch created a more sombre occasion. Despite the workload, however, there were many compensations. Among them were the tours in the civil engineer's saloon, useful and fascinating, but quite stressful when the general manager was with us, and hours of preparing for his barrage of questions never quite covered all the bases.

One memory that will never leave me is that of a visit to the Sudbrook Pumping station, which housed the machinery that kept the Severn Tunnel dry. The tunnel had been inundated several times during construction, both by the River Severn itself and by the waters of the Great Spring, a subterranean flow breached by the early tun-nelling works. The 4.35-mile bore, sited near the present motorway crossings of the estuary, slopes down from each shore to pass beneath a deep river channel known as The Shoots. Not only does water drain down the slope from the surrounding land but, with the addition of that of the Great Spring, something like 28 million gallons has to be pumped clear every day. Originally this was done by massive beam engines powered by a long rank of Cornish boilers. Although electri-cal pumps had taken over by the time of my visit, the beams were still there. They impressed me greatly, as did a descent to the tunnel proper, with the flow of the Great Spring running in a channel beneath my feet. Another river crossing, that by the Severn Railway Bridge, fared less well during my Bristol period for it was run into by tanker barges, resulting in two spans collapsing and eventual demolition.

The people I worked with were a grand, able and enterprising bunch and our annual divisional dinners most pleasant occasions. Admittedly, because of my habit of collecting railway relics and ephemera, I was surprised with the presentation of a GWR toilet seat at one of these gatherings, but the main perpetrator woke up the following Sunday to find the huge porcelain WC pan in his front garden. Revenge was sweet!

THE MOBILE
COMMAND POST

'It seemed like a good idea', but then, when the time came, Philip Benham's command post was forgotten

When a major incident occurs on the railway, such as a derailment, arrangements are needed on site for co-ordinating action and managing the recovery process. These days such command and control processes are highly organised, with modern communications facilities and specialist response vehicles from the emergency services and others capable of rapid deployment.

Back in the 1970s matters were less well developed. An accident could occur anywhere, and gaining access to site could be a challenge in itself at some of the more remote locations. Once on site, there would probably be little, if any, communications – mobile phones were a technology still some way off – and almost certainly there would be little in the way of facilities for those trying to manage the incident.

This very real problem had exercised the minds of the London Midland Region's senior operating people, and someone had come up with an idea. The plan was for each of the region's seven divisions to have a tent built into a trailer of a type quite popular at the time with campers. The trailer was to be kept at a suitable central point and, when needed, would simply be towed to site and erected. In the Nottingham Division this would be a job for divisional inspectors like me.

It was realised that in an emergency, time would be of the essence, so we inspectors needed to know the drill and to be able to reach the site and erect the tent in the minimum of time. Not being one of life's 'great outdoors' types, and my colleagues were not either, practise was needed. Thus every now and again we would take the command post for a 'spin' and practise erecting the tent at a suitable location, timing our efforts. Generally this was considered a great sport and was a change from the normal routine, although quite how two of the other inspectors managed to overturn the trailer on the main road outside Ratcliffe-on-Soar power station we will never know.

History suggests that although the command posts were deployed in earnest, in practice they were of limited value. The immediate demands following an incident, and the better facilities of the emergency services, usually meant that the command post trailer was something of a white elephant.

On one occasion an exercise was set up using the largely redundant Chaddesden Sidings near Derby. All the emergency services were involved in working with railway officers to test response to a simulated major passenger train derailment. Peter Aitkin, another inspector, and I were deputed to wait in Derby Power Box with the command post trailer until called. The brief was that we should then make our way to site as quickly as possible and erect the tent to act as a command post for the operations officer in charge.

The hour arrived and Peter and I dutifully awaited the call. Time passed, minutes turning into hours. Eventually we learnt the exercise was over, but what of the command post? The explanation was simple, Control had forgotten to call us, and no one on site had felt it necessary to ask where we were!

LINCOLNSHIRE AND DR BEECHING

In the 1960–70s purge on lightly used railways, the whole of East Lincolnshire featured prominently in the scrutiny and closure process, and Bryan Stone was in the thick of it

This is heavyweight stuff. In my collection is a thick, heavy, green-covered book entitled, *Proposed Withdrawal of Passenger Services, Peterborough–Spalding–Boston, Firsby (Inclusive)–Grimsby, Willoughby–Mablethorpe, Lincoln (Central)–Skegness (via Midville)*. It details closure proposals for 106 miles of route, and nineteen stations, one of which, Tumby Woodside, was immortalised in Flanders' and Swann's song 'Slow Train'. The book is dated October 1967, several hundred copies were sent out, and it was all prepared by two clerks in my little 'Special Duties Section, Re-Shaping' which had a room in the tower

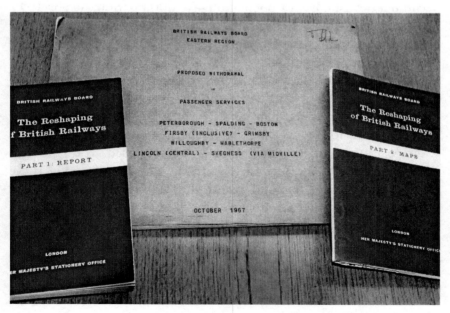

'The Beeching Report' and line closure proposals in the eastern part of Lincolnshire. (Bryan Stone)

of Lincoln Central station. I was passenger manager in Doncaster, and this was part of my responsibility. They were a hardworking pair, on borrowed time and working themselves out of a job. This one, however, was a big proposal, and went under the name of the 'East Lincolnshire Closures'. It is worth thinking about what was going on, for today 'Beeching' is a synonym scornfully used for railway closures without any idea of what was expected of him or us.

The GNR, MSLR/GCR, Midland and M&GN railways all once served Lincolnshire's agriculture, industries and coastline, thought to be a honey pot. Remember the grandly named Ambergate, Nottingham, Boston & Eastern Junction Railway? There were others. The East Lincolnshire line, properly speaking, was the one from Peterborough through Boston and Louth to Grimsby. Its role in history was assured; the first Great Northern Railway trains ran at its northern end, two years before the main line through Grantham and Retford was opened, and the first GNR London–York trains ran through Boston and Lincoln to Doncaster.

The Lincolnshire of 1960 was, however, not that of 1848. Boston had once been second to London as a trading port, but was rapidly declining. Grimsby, from a population of 1,000 in 1800, had by 1912 become, partly thanks to the railways, the biggest fishing port in the country, and had reached a population of 100,000. The legendary fish trains were just ending.

Line closures in Lincolnshire were not new. Some once-prosperous branches, like those to Horncastle and Spilsby, and doubtful cases like Louth to Lincoln via Bardney, and Louth to Mablethorpe, were long gone. Sleaford to Bourne had closed to passengers in 1931! Many wayside stations on through lines had also closed. The RAF and USAAF airfields in the Second World War had given some of these a last bonus of peak demand, before they finally went to sleep. My little Lincoln office had just prepared the closure of our portion of the M&GN and the Grimsby & Immingham Light Railway.

Now we had Dr Beeching and the *Re-Shaping of British Railways*, the Blue Book, published in 1963. He was not there to destroy railways, but by governmental order, under the Transport Act of 1962, to reshape railways for a new, and uncertain, future. I was thus part of a national process, with its own line of command from the Ministry of Transport, through the British Railways Board, to its regions and

A Lincoln-bound diesel multiple unit at Stixwould station, empty of people and separated from its village by the River Witham. (Bryan Stone)

districts, because the order was, 'If it is listed in the Blue Book for closure, prepare a submission (i.e. locally). This will be appraised in accordance with the Act at government (MoT) level.'

Neither we nor Beeching could close anything without going through the prescribed consultation procedure. This cut right across normal management structures and gave us little room to wriggle. Progress meetings were chaired by a BRB representative. However, wriggle we did. I was convinced that the various Lincolnshire lines were insufficiently differentiated. There were several hopeless cases, but some errors and omissions on the Blue Book's maps helped to open a debate. So did a major project completed in 1965, the south to east curve at Newark Midland Crossing. This would prove to be the key to re-launching passenger service in Lincolnshire. The Beeching Report ignored it. Lincoln–Nottingham was down for closure. It was reprieved, and is still there.

The hugely expensive East Lincolnshire route, together with the branches east of Lincoln, all in that big green-covered book, could not be reprieved. Yet there was a snag. Two Cleethorpes–London expresses ran daily each way, and these were a prestige job. If Sir Cyril Osborne, then Conservative MP for Louth (South). and many others could not travel to parliament and breakfast on 'the London train', we were 'in for it'. Well, Sir Cyril did his best, and I was an obvious target.

Then fortune smiled again. I found an old Great Central Railway passenger timetable of 1922. This showed the services across north Lincolnshire, from Sheffield to Lincoln, Scunthorpe, Grimsby and New Holland, of forty years earlier. They were still operating, after the Depression, world war and nationalisation, almost identically in 1964, even with diesel multiple units (DMUs), often in the same paths. Could that really be right? And could we really cut off Grimsby (now a big complex with Immingham) and Lincoln, with another 100,000 people, from the main line? Existing traffics, very fragmented, were clearly a poor guide. On that basis we deserved to have it all closed down. Just suppose we tried to do better?

I needed some friends. The regional passenger manager thought it worth a try. My divisional manager, Fred Wright, gave me a free hand, as long as the East Lincolnshire proposal was not delayed. I could respect that. We quickly found that a regular interval service of semi-fasts could be put in, with our DMUs, between Sheffield and Doncaster, Scunthorpe and Grimsby, and between Grimsby, the Market Rasen line, Lincoln and Newark Northgate (by the new curve). We got connections into the new regular main line semi-fasts at Newark, another stroke of luck because the East Coast Main Line operation was really out of my class! We showed that regular, tightly timed services would save time, staff and several of around forty-eight DMU diagrams then operated from Lincoln depot. We got more train miles and much better services, with fewer train sets. New diagrams from HQ came out, consultation went through, and a new Lincolnshire timetable became public reality.

The new timetable gave demonstrable improvements to Grimsby, Lincoln and Scunthorpe, some 300,000 people, and the London trains re-routed via Lincoln and Newark direct to King's Cross were a bonus. There really were more passengers, and more receipts, though Lincolnshire railways would never be truly profitable. We got some things wrong. There were inevitably some compromises. The uproar at Louth and Boston was foreseeable, but the East Lincolnshire was clearly redundant. Pending closure (which came five years later), Louth got a connection into the expresses, and Boston a DMU link

Spalding station, formerly an important interchange point between the M&GN, GN&GE Joint and East Lincolnshire lines. (Bryan Stone)

At Firsby, passengers alight from an East Lincs line service, watched by the driver of the Skegness branch train in the adjacent platform. (Bryan Stone)

to Spalding and Peterborough. I had some exciting meetings with local authorities, with Sir Cyril, and with the *Lincolnshire Standard*, but everyone knew that it could not last. Some stations like Appleby (Lincs), not on Beeching's lists, were also shown to be irrelevant.

I would have closed the Barnetby–Gainsborough Central service, which added little, but HQ said no. Well, it didn't prosper. But we had to get on with the closure proposals. My little Lincoln office spent months looking at alternative bus services, often far inferior to the minimal number of trains, for the few local passengers. Most painful for me, were the staff meetings. There were many staff at signal boxes and level crossings who had no future, and there was no work in East Lincolnshire, except down on the farm. What good was offering a job in Scunthorpe or Lincoln, to a signalman in Willoughby? And yet they knew it had to be, and I went home often a sadder and a wiser man.

It is now fifty years later, and today I know that sectorisation and privatisation have made hay with what we did. Most of the East Lincolnshire was closed in 1970, although Skegness was kept. The Grimsby–London trains finally fell foul of East Coast electrification. The Lincoln–Newarks remained and gave the London connections. And at least we had shown, as today's map confirms, that we could do better than the raw plan; the people came and used the new trains, and the MoT and the BRB (British Railway Board) left things alone.

TAILPIECE

Part of this proposal was the Mablethorpe branch. In summer this could be busy, and excursions ran. In winter there were few passengers. Chris Smith, my head of section, would come to me to say, not unusually, that we were short of a Lincoln diagram DMU. First choice for a substitute bus was usually the Mablethorpe branch. However, there were times, like in February, when we only ordered a taxi, and even then we would learn that no one was there waiting. So much for popular demand!

A STROKE OF LUCK AT MILNGAVIE JUNCTION

**Instinct and good fortune served Hugh Gould well and
saved his driver from serious consequences**

In the summer of 1955, when I was a passenger guard at Hyndland,
we sometimes covered duties at some of the smaller depots in the
Glasgow South district, such as Kirkintilloch and Shettleston.

On 8 August I was rostered for the solitary Shettleston turn starting with the 7.34 Shettleston to Dalmuir, headed by Parkhead depot's
prize Class V3 tank engine No. 67655, gleaming like a new pin as
always. This was despite the absence today of the regular driver, Bill
Turnbull, whom I knew well and whose keen attention to his work
was the reason for the gleam.

We ran normally until approaching Westerton, when a slight hesitation indicated that although the Milngavie Junction Home signal
had cleared, the Starting signal some distance beyond Westerton station might not have done so. On pulling away from Westerton, something told me to check that the Starter was 'off'. I looked out to see
67655 steaming cheerfully away past the signal which was definitely
'on'! I lunged for the brake and we ground to a halt with only a small
part of the train on the right side of the signal.

I walked back to Milngavie Junction signal box to 'sign in' and make
peace with the signalman. No less than eleven minutes then elapsed
before we 'got the road', but I never found out why. When we got to
Dalmuir, the driver came rushing back to express his gratitude. I went
home that day feeling insufferably righteous, and have often wondered
what might have happened!

EUROSTAR STORY

**Peter Whitaker played a major part in the pioneering
beginnings of the Eurostar activity in the 1990s**

As director of personnel policy at BRB Headquarters I discovered
that, like many BR directors, I was not able to 'direct' very much,
and that if we had a personnel policy it was not easy to identify or
to redefine. Accordingly, when the then managing director, personnel, said something on the lines of: 'The Channel Tunnel lot will be
moving from a project team to a company and will be needing a personnel director and would you be interested?' It took very little time
indeed for me to respond: 'When do I start?'

However, I then found that my appointment had to be approved by
the redoubtable John Palmer, a hardened Department of Transport
veteran, who had become chairman of the emerging 'Channel Tunnel'
organisation. He was clearly somewhat sceptical about the ability of an
experienced BR practitioner to switch to the radical, creative approach
he felt was necessary. When I asked him about contracts and conditions
of employment, the answer was 'a blank sheet of paper for you to work
on.' An opportunity only dreamed about for so many frustrating years!

The following week a grand meeting took place in the august halls of
222 Marylebone Road with all the railway trade union leaders, clearing the ground for the European Passenger Services (EPS) organisation to take the lead in developing agreed employment arrangements.
As I left the room I felt a hand on my shoulder and Lew Adams of the
Associated Society of Locomotive Engineers & Firemen (ASLEF) whispered, 'We want to be part of this. As long as you don't push us too
hard we will be with you.' Later he proved to be as good as his word, of
which more anon.

When I joined the organisation much of the groundwork had
already been laid, notably by Malcolm Southgate and Alec Bath and
others, and latterly by Richard Edgley the newly appointed managing director. The intellectual and analytical (but results and perfor-
mance focussed) Richard and the vastly experienced, wise, massively
calm and people-friendly (especially French people!) Malcolm were an
inspired combination. Most of us in senior positions in this new team

80

were in traditional orthodox BR terms over-qualified for our roles but, far from 'coasting' or adopting dyed-in-the-wool approaches, we used our bedrock of experience as a strength and rose to the challenge and the opportunity we were offered.

Apart from the huge challenges of delivering the infrastructure, trains, working arrangements and agreements with Eurotunnel, SNCF, SNCB, Network South East and others, we needed to recruit, train and motivate a new workforce. Our recruitment and selection methods were 'leading edge' for the time. Led by Alec Bath, we developed a partnership with a consortium of London Polytechnics to deliver French language tuition to the train drivers, an essential operational requirement. Not one driver failed the stringent final test. Under the leadership of the engineering director, Mike Etwell, the training and development of maintenance staff set new standards. Customer service was at the forefront of our agenda and our customer interface staff were similarly trained to very high standards.

The key element of the employment 'package' was an annual hours contract, at that time still comparatively rare in this country. We had researched other UK employers and the approaches of other railway companies, notably NS (Nederlandse Spoorwegen, the principal passenger railway operator in the Netherlands), but this concept was still novel – and certainly to our trade union friends! In essence *all* staff were to be salaried and committed to working flexible hours. Not only did we see this as the right long-term basis, but anything less would have entailed train crews especially being extremely unproductive and expensive in terms of the emerging timetable requirements.

In addition to gaining understanding of the concept, and putting some definition on maximum hours, leave entitlements etc., the key element was to achieve sufficiently attractive salary levels in effect to 'buy out' traditional overtime, rest day and leave expectations. Here we were under the most intense scrutiny from Railways Board level, since it was realised that we would be setting possibly damaging precedents for the soon-to-be-privatised train-operating companies.

All this was against the background of an EPS board decision that trade unions would not be 'recognised'. Inevitably, this meant a lengthy and tortuous process of discussions with the trade unions, all against a looming deadline of start of services, with recruitment and the long training of train drivers very much on the critical path. It all led to the traditional overnight jamboree when, by the middle of Friday after-noon, it was clear that the RMT (National Union of Rail, Maritime and Transport Workers) representatives were not going to reach agreement with us.

Then, by a strange coincidence(!), Lew Adams and I found it neces-sary to retire to the 'Gents' at the same time and subsequently to take a walk in the car park together. After that, Lew returned to the meeting room and told all concerned that ASLEF would accept our final offer and, in effect, if RMT did not like it they knew what they could do!

I subsequently had a very sleepless night imagining the red-top headlines on the salary levels I had agreed. On the Monday morning I had an uncomfortable board meeting explaining why it had been pru-dent and necessary to move beyond our previously agreed 'best offer' to achieve a full settlement. So, what we had achieved: effectively, full commitment to annual hours with overtime to be paid only in excep-tional circumstances; full acceptance of our proposed recruitment and training including French tuition for train drivers and, we had success-fully walked a tricky tightrope of consultation whilst stopping short of formal union recognition.

The train drivers and other staff were duly recruited and success-fully trained and the Queen and President Mitterand were able to open the Channel Tunnel formally with the participation of Eurostar trains (much sticking plaster and fuse wire!) on 6 May 1994.

The managing director, introducing me to Her Majesty on that occa-sion said: 'This is our personnel director.'

Her Majesty then said to yours truly: 'And what does that involve?'

I answered: 'Well your Majesty ... !'

SHIP AHOY

Jim Summers describes the occasion when what should have been a prestige occasion for a brand new vessel turned into a bit of a drama

The brand new ship lay at the buoys out in the river awaiting her first voyage. She had been named in the new unimaginative, un-poetic style,

Early days at Parkeston Container Terminal with *Seafreighter II* beneath one of the Goliath cranes and the older container ship *Colchester* on the left. (Jim Summers)

which reduced otherwise decent self-respecting ships into dismal numbers, like *Holyhead Ferry I*. In this case, the newly delivered vessel was *Seafreightliner II*, and she lay ahead of the more romantically named *Amsterdam*. Her elder sister – you've guessed it: *Seafreightliner I* – had recently opened the Parkeston Quay–Zeebrugge container service very effectively, and the two ships were now to operate an intensive service. But there was also to be a Rotterdam service, and *SFII*, being shiny and new, was to open it. By contrast, her mate out at the buoys in the river, old *Amsterdam*, was tired and at the end of her life. She had been withdrawn recently from the Parkeston Quay–Hoek van Holland overnight run, and was awaiting her final sad, empty voyage to the breakers. She had only a watchman aboard, but the crew of *SFII* were all present and shipshape fashion, 'rarin' to go'. Unlike the graceful old steamer moored ahead, they had all mod. cons, not least bridge control of the engines. With his own hands, the master could drive the ship from the bridge, without any telegraphing down to the engine room.

So it was that, with the intention of manoeuvring the ship from the middle of the river to a berth alongside the container terminal for its first cargo, Captain M. let in the clutch, as it were, with a feeling of pride and anticipation. The effect was not quite what he anticipated. The ship shot forward uncontrollably and cut the cables securing the *Amsterdam* to her buoy. The buoy passed below *SFII*, and shot into the air.

The lonely watchman aboard *Amsterdam* realised his ship was now adrift and he was indeed alone without steam up. Meanwhile *SFII*, having careered about, ended her voyage with some initiative by crashing into the quay. The resultant scorecard was one new and expensively damaged ship, no opening of the new container service, a graceful old lady being chased by a tug in the river, a red-faced ship's master, and an awful lot of paperwork.

The most galling thing about it all, was that I had been on night shift and colleagues only told me about the dramatic occasion afterwards, but in my dreams I did seem to hear an awful lot of ships' whistles!

AREA MOVEMENTS INSPECTOR

It was unheard of for ex-management trainees to go straight into operating inspector posts but Chris Blackman broke the mould and got his bowler

On finishing management training in September 1969, I was appointed area movements inspector (AMI) in the Willesden Area with particular responsibility for thirty-four signal boxes. This was a somewhat terrifying proposition for someone with just two years' experience. Later I found out that the London Euston divisional operating superintendent (DOS), Sid Keeling, had been urging the Regional Training Committee to appoint an ex-trainee to a DI (district inspector) or AMI post, but this had been resisted on the grounds that more experience than two years as a trainee was required. By 1969 there was a dearth of suitable assistant area manager jobs at Supervisory Grade C, and the Training Committee reluctantly agreed, as an experiment, to do a trial appointment of an ex-trainee to a DI/AMI post. However, they took the precaution of declaring that this should take place in Sid Keeling's division. The sub text, of course, was that 'on his head be it!'

Willesden Area had such a vacancy for an AMI, and I duly reported for duty on 8 September to meet Area Manager Frank Sykes. Before I sat down he told me bluntly that it was totally inappropriate for an ex-trainee to be appointed to such a job. He was at pains to tell me that he himself had been a DI, but only after years of studying the rules and regulations and with a wealth of experience under his belt. He added that he was going to get it changed and would have a word with the divisional office to sort out something more suitable. I waited outside with a growing lack of confidence. A little later I was told that my appointment would proceed. I gathered subsequently that Sykes's conversation with Sid Keeling had not lasted long, nor did his appointment as area manager at Willesden, as he moved to Crewe six weeks later.

Eric Ball arrived as area manager shortly after. He also had been a DI, but didn't bang on about it; he simply gave me every encouragement, was always ready to offer advice if asked, but left me alone to get on with my duties. As an experienced railwayman he had many contacts and knew how to tap into the grapevine, so would have monitored my progress discreetly. I have always been grateful to him.

Willesden Area had, at the beginning of that September, taken over the old Broad Street Area, so it stretched from Dalston East (interface with Victoria Park on the Eastern Region) to Kew East (interface with the Southern at Old Kew and New Kew) and from Broad Street to Willesden Carriage Shed North. The new post of AMI in effect replaced that of the old district inspector, so I was proud to be a DI, albeit very young and inexperienced. Naturally, I wore the traditional 'black Mac' as issued, and even went out and bought a trilby.

I had about three weeks' familiarisation with the area in the company of Tommy Page, who then went off to be AMI in the Marylebone area. I also spent a day working West Hendon box under the watchful eye of St Pancras AMI Norman Fletton. Then it was in at the deep end. Four weeks later I had a message from the DOS's office to meet Sid Keeling at Camden Road station. We had a chat; he seemed content with reports on progress so far, but was not impressed by the trilby. 'Get yourself a bowler hat,' he insisted. You don't argue with the DOS, so I paid another visit to the hat shop. The bowler was only used if I knew Sid was going to be around or if we had a visit from the general manager – Bobby Lawrence – doing a grand tour of the newly enlarged Willesden Area or an inspecting officer from Her Majesty's Railway Inspectorate (HMRI) – Maj. Peter Olver – to inspect Bollo Lane Junction alterations or a Royal Train.

Years later, just before I retired in 2007, when I was the secretary of the Access Disputes Committee, I was officiating as returning officer at the election of the committee representative for one of the passenger classes when there was a tie of votes cast. The election was decided by drawing lots out of a hat, so the bowler came out of the cupboard to perform its final duty!

MORE BOWLER HATS

Former district inspectors Geoff Briggs and Jan Glasscock, along with Jim Summers, recount incidents which reveal something of the variety of their jobs

Geoff Briggs recalls:

When I was the Doncaster chief divisional inspector and 'on call', I was asked to go out to Potteric Carr signal box as a report had been received of a horse on the line. On arrival at the box there was no sign of the signalman or of the horse. After a while the signalman appeared out of the darkness. I asked him where he had been all the time that I'd been looking for him. 'Where have I been?' he said. 'I've been out there in the black night looking for a b**** black horse! You'd have been out there a b**** long time, too!'

During my tenure a vast new coal mine north of Selby meant the diversion of the East Coast Main Line in order to facilitate mining and avoid any adverse effect on train services. This was the first new railway in the UK to be built specifically for running at 125mph.

The diversion was opened in sections, the final part being from Hambleton Junction to Colton Junction, south of York. The new track top was well rusted and could not be relied upon to operate track circuits. It was decided, therefore, to run merry-go-round coal trains (meaning they were loaded and unloaded simultaneously whilst moving) over the line under the supervision of the divisional chief inspector until it was felt safe for passenger services.

I watched operations from the recently installed 'NX' panel in the old York signal box, and things wwent so well that I was able to authorise passenger services over the diversion much earlier than had been anticipated. After talking with Doncaster power box signalman, this was agreed.

Unknown to me there was a parallel plan for the top brass at York to travel on the first train, which was expected to be later in the day. To my dismay, I learned from Regional Control that the top brass could be seen 'jumping out of taxis and running frantically to the station so as not to miss the inaugural train!'

THE BEST LAID PLANS!

Jan Glasscock was a district inspector in the King's Cross operating district in the 1960s and when snow was expected, DI cover had to be provided round the clock at Hornsey Up Goods signal box. This was to ensure uninterrupted movements of the many trains of empty coaches which ran from Hornsey carriage sidings to King's Cross. Of such an occasion he records:

One cold January day, it fell to me to do the 6 p.m. to 6 a.m. duty at Hornsey Up Goods signal box. I approached across the tracks just after a set of empty coaches departed from the sidings. The route was under a high gantry on top of which were several signals on separate posts, including one with three miniature signals in a vertical line. The district inspector I was going to relieve had climbed up the walkway of the gantry and then up another ladder to reach one of these which had stuck in the off position after the last movement. Having knocked the offending signal back into place he gingerly retraced his route down amid falling shards of snow and ice.

Watching the precarious progress, I said to the signalman, who was well known to me, 'Have I really got to do that?'

He looked at me knowingly, and said, 'He gets right up my nose; but don't worry, that one always sticks off and I've brought trains out that way all day to get him out of the box as much as possible. Now that you're here, I'll bring them out another way.'

Needless to say, I had an uneventful night with no trips outside to climb up signal gantries.

In 1968 we had a period of booked single-line working on Saturday nights over the Down line between Yaxley and Home for engineering work. In those days several Up sleeping car trains ran over the ECML early on Sunday mornings, were crossed over at Yaxley, ran in both directions under the pilotman's authority, and then crossed back over to the Up line at Holme. Early one particular morning, I had to ride with the driver of one of these sleeping car trains to bring back a Down train from Holme. Having reversed over the trailing crossover at Yaxley on to the Down line and assured myself all was in order to proceed, I instructed the guard and driver, and we set off in the wrong direction to Holme.

The next signal to be obeyed was the Holme Up Distant, and then the Outer Holme, some considerable distance away. There were no facing points or catch points in the single line and the driver had the controller of the Deltic locomotive full open. After a short while I checked the speedometer – we were doing 75mph! Although no limit was laid down that, by any standards over a single line in the wrong direction, was too fast.

I said to the driver, something like, 'Steady on mate, I think you're going a bit hard.'

He turned and looked at me and said, as only drivers can, 'The speed in the right direction is 85mph. The Rule Book says I should travel over the single line in the wrong direction at reduced speed – and this is reduced speed!'

A further discussion followed, upon which the speed was reduced considerably!

Jim Summers recalls one occasion when it seemed a good idea to take the up-and-coming young head shunter along to the district inspector's evening classes on rules and regulations. It also seemed a good and friendly idea to seat him between the assistant yard master and yard inspector on his first night at the classes:

The DI was expanding on single-line working and, in particular, on the rule requiring the pilotman to be present to authorise any movements on to the single line. 'Any movement whatever,' he emphasised.

A main line separated the two local yards and, with memories of a bout of single-line working on that main line, the keen young shunter made bold to offer a question, 'But surely it is OK if the pilotman is not there and you are only taking a few wagons from a yard across to the other ... ' The question tailed off, as he was abruptly dug in the ribs from both sides.

'Maybe I could discuss that point with you afterwards,' said the DI, with a meaningful look towards the two old lags, now gazing intently at the ceiling.

THE AWAKENING

Some exciting new ideas were tried to increase passenger travel in David Jagoe's time in the WR Cardiff Division

Following the excitement of the British Empire Games in 1958, in which the Cardiff Division had a very important role to play in organising the total transport logistics, the rail passenger activity settled down into a routine of an hourly service from Swansea, Bridgend, Cardiff and Newport to London, services to Bristol and the South West, two services to the Midlands, the Valleys commuter services and the football and rugby specials. The football specials always required a police dog and handler, not required on the rugby specials!

The passenger business had become static, even moribund, and the need to raise awareness and awaken interest in rail travel was recognised. So, in 1990, a number of initiatives were introduced to meet the challenge of 'putting more bums on seats'.

To test 'the temperature of the water' in the leisure travel sector, Mystery Trips were trial marketed using the spare capacity of the Valley commuter DMUs. A limited programme of trips to local destinations such as Tenby and Fishguard was researched, in conjunction with the local authorities to ensure that facilities would be available. They were introduced on Sundays to avoid clashes with football, rugby or family shopping (at that time Sundays were still regarded as 'hallowed'). The response exceeded all expectations, and quickly led to expanding the product into English destinations, employing available main line resources. Once again each destination was carefully researched, guided by the appropriate BR Division and local community organisations, in order to ensure that facilities would be available on the day. A measure of the success was the increase in demand from one to two trains each weekend, and the very high retention rate of customers as groups of trippers formed their own 'clubs' and pre-booked future excursions in advance, and the total absence of complaints even if they were returned to the same destination a week later.

To remove the pressure on the booking offices and to expand the scope of rail-based travel, travel agency styled travel centres were successfully introduced at each of the principal main line stations, offering travel advice, pre-booking arrangements and taking on the responsibility of servicing the local travel agents. One member of the sales team was retained to focus solely on Group Travel through working men's clubs, miners' clubs, sport clubs, church groups and schools. With the right person in place, this closely focused approach yielded a lucrative dividend.

More by 'gut feeling' than any constructive logic, telephone selling – still in its infancy as a marketing tool – was introduced. Two ladies were appointed following interviews conducted on the telephone and were trained by the Institute of Marketing. On their return, their task was to research professional conferences and exhibitions and, by contacting senior executive managers in each appropriate group, sell them rail travel and accommodation with the Metropolitan Hotel Group. Success of the project was measured by the large majority of executives approached who appreciated the contact and the extent to which a great many took advantage of it, making advance bookings and in some cases group bookings. The cherry on the cake was an irate Leo Abse, MP and local solicitor, who rang the divisional manager complaining that he had been reached in person at his office telephone by one of these calls. He was advised that that was regarded as the objective of the process and perhaps he should have a word with his secretary.

A proposal from Regional HQ to enhance the hourly London service by increasing it to half-hourly was firmly rejected, mainly on

At Cardiff Queen Street, the 14.36 to Bridgend via the Vale of Glamorgan is due to depart in three minutes while the Cardiff Bay shuttle stands in the other platform. (Ian Body)

the grounds that long-distance travel was not a speculative business, but required pre-arrangement, and that demographic research of the South Wales population clearly demonstrated that only a very small sector would be in a position to take advantage of rail travel during weekdays after 9 a.m. The only group that might respond was the wives of businessmen – who could join their husbands who had travelled up on the earlier Pullman services – as they were the only ones with the available time and cash, but they would need an exciting or interesting motive to travel to London. The Metropolitan Hotel Group and a number of West End theatres were approached and agreed to co-operate with discounted tariffs.

For this potential business a number of packages were developed, one employing one of the two 'Club Cars' acquired by the region. Avon Cosmetics, with their plant in Bridgend, were more than willing to make available beauty consultants on a daily basis for a month on a mid-morning 'Coffee Express', with Marks and Spencer agreeing to follow on. For subsequent services, a 'Lunch Special' and later in the day an 'Afternoon Tea Special', all at attractive prices, were planned. In the end and after all the endeavour and painstakingly detailed planning to create a novel approach to rail travel, Regional HQ decided that the two 'Club Cars' should be allocated instead to the Bristol services.

Although this exciting and novel approach to increasing business on the very lightly loaded London service had fallen at the last hurdle, the other initiatives were certainly regarded as having raised the profile and awakened interest in rail travel in South Wales.

WHO ARE YOU ANYWAY?

**A stressful day was going well until Terry Worrall
failed to recognise the BRB Chief Executive**

In 1981, during my tenure as Area Manager London Bridge, I was advised by the Southern Region HQ public relations officer that my area had been chosen, as one of the busiest commuter areas in London, to host an early morning visit to London Bridge station, by the then Government Transport Minister, David Howell, and his entourage. They would be accompanied by representatives from the British Railways Board and senior SR officers, including the general manager, David Kirby, his regional operations manager and Bob Newlyn, the South Eastern Divisional Manager.

In those days the main day-to-day area operational matters were handled between the area and the divisional staff. It would be rare that an area manager would have direct dealings with regional head-quarters and even more rare to have dealings with anyone from the BRB. During the visit I would be expected to have ready answers in order to respond to questions and to conduct the visit to the operating floor of London Bridge panel signal box (PSB), which was acknowledged as being the busiest PSB on the BR system at that time. I was advised that the group would also wish to see the technical side of the PSB and that Cliff Hale, the regional signalling and telecommunications manager, was expected to conduct that part of the visit. Prior to the visit, Cliff and I liaised to make sure that our respective presentations were complementary, with mine focusing on the operational aspects and his upon the technical ones.

Came the day and at 8 a.m. the party arrived on the Central side of London Bridge station to observe commuters arriving in great numbers, the party itself numbering about fifteen. After this, and some discussion about the 'peak problems' and activities, I led the group to the PSB, where I gave my introduction on the operating floor, introducing signalmen and supervisors as I did so. This went without a hitch.

We then retired to the ground floor and went into the relay room where Cliff Hale started his presentation. As he was talking an individual at the back of the group interjected several times saying, 'Make sure you tell the minister about ...' He said this four or five times, and was starting to put Cliff off his stroke.

I turned round, no doubt with a sign of irritation, and suggested that this individual desist from his interruptions, leaving any points he wished to make until the end. I also asked him, 'Who are you anyway?'

'Reid – Chief Executive BRB,' he responded.

I was almost speechless, although I managed to get out a rather tame, 'I should have recognised you from your picture in *Rail News.*' In my horror at not realising this was the top man of our industry, it was the only thing I could think of saying.

My divisional manager and others who overheard this exchange were quietly amused and no doubt expected some strong follow-up, as did I, but it was my good fortune that there was none. How lucky I was!

ROBBING PETER

A clever move by Philip Benham to facilitate the chairman's inspection of a new automated enquiry office at York backfired slightly

In 1984 a long-overdue programme was underway to replace the booking and enquiry offices at York station, badly damaged by wartime bombing, with a new travel centre. During the building work, ticket selling and enquiry work was housed in a two-storey Portakabin in the station forecourt. This was in the days before the large call centres we are all so familiar with today, and telephone enquiries about train times and fares were still handled locally. So while passengers were attended to

The enquiry office at York station. (Philip Benham)

downstairs, the top floor was given over to the telephone bureau – where the volume of calls usually required three to four staff to be on duty.

The British Rail Chairman, Sir Robert Reid, was due to pay one of his periodic 'state visits' to Eastern Region headquarters, also located in York, offering an ideal opportunity to show off the work taking place at the station. As the local area manager, I was to accompany Deputy General Manager Colin Driver on the tour of inspection and explain the work taking place.

The chairman's visit was scheduled for a Friday afternoon in the height of summer. Shortly before the due time, I carried out a quick recce of the route with Station Manager Jim Collins, to ensure all was well – it was never wise to leave such visits to chance, especially with Sir Robert, who would not be slow in expressing his views if anything amiss was found. Friday was always busy, especially in summer, and passenger numbers were boiling up nicely. Downstairs in the temporary office, queues were beginning to stretch out of the doors into the forecourt. This did not give a good impression, and the travel centre manager was told to make sure there were plenty of staff deployed to keep as many ticket and enquiry positions open as possible.

The visit took place a short time later. The chairman seemed impressed with the building work, and had visited the temporary office where the extra staff drafted to the front line were keeping the queues nicely under control. He would be on his way shortly, and then we could all relax a little. What else was there to see? 'How about the telephone enquiry office, upstairs?' says Colin. So up we go and through the door to the office. There we are greeted by the strident ringing of several unanswered telephones. They were unanswered because there was not a soul to be seen. True to my request, the travel centre manager had indeed ensured there were plenty of enquiry clerks downstairs – by drawing everyone out of the telephone bureau!

Horrified, I decided my best action was to busy myself answering one of the phones, while Jim hurried off to find some staff. The chairman looked bemused, but it was a Friday afternoon, and generally he must have been impressed with his visit to the region, as he seemed to accept my lame explanation of staff shortage complicated by the loss of flexibility caused by the building work.

Jim Collins went on to be personal assistant to Sir Robert Reid, but to the best of my knowledge he never mentioned the day we introduced BR's first fully automated telephone enquiry bureau.

ROYAL RECALL

**Area Manager Harold Forster found meeting people
at Manchester Piccadilly 'fun, fulfilling and very
satisfying', and learned a lesson from a much-loved
member of the Royal Family**

It is probably true to say that there can be no better stage upon which to meet people than that provided by a large railway passenger station. It was my good fortune, for over fourteen years, to enjoy the privilege of meeting all kinds of people on the platforms of Manchester Piccadilly station and, reflecting on those often quick and chance encounters, it is surprising to recognise just how much they taught me.

It was no less than Her Royal Highness the Queen Mother who convinced me that there is danger in making unfounded assumptions.

On one occasion when she visited Manchester things did not go entirely to plan. For some reason, to my great horror, the door from which the Queen Mother alighted did not coincide with the carefully laid red carpet on the platform! However, Her Royal Highness, charming and friendly as always, made no comment and I assumed that maybe she had not noticed our gaffe.

How wrong that assumption proved was clearly emphasised some twelve months later when the same royal personage made another visit to Manchester. This time, thankfully, the carpet was in the appropriate place, a fact obviously noticed by the Queen Mother who, with a sly grin, quietly said, 'You've made it this time!'

Maybe this experience was not new to her, but the need to be careful in making assumptions had come to me from no less a source than a revered member of the Royal Family.

EARL MOUNTBATTEN'S FUNERAL TRAIN

Mike Phillips recounts the events of Wednesday 5 September 1979 when a special train carried the earl's coffin for burial at Romsey Abbey

Earl Mountbatten of Burma had been assassinated while on holiday in Northern Ireland by terrorist action. For many years, he had expressed the wish that, upon his death, his body would be conveyed to Romsey in Hampshire. And thus it was that, following his tragic death, the railway was entrusted with the arrangements to carry out his wishes.

It is a well-known that any events associated with members of the Royal Family are meticulously planned to the last detail. It is, therefore, no surprise that for a number of years there had been meetings at Southern Region Headquarters at Waterloo station to discuss and confirm the arrangements for a special train to operate as part of the funeral ceremony. This would convey the Royal Family and mourners, along with the earl's coffin, from Waterloo to Romsey for transfer from the station there to Romsey Abbey. The route to be taken by the train was over the former London & South Western main line and totally under the operational jurisdiction of the divisional manager based at Wimbledon. Direct control of the route passed to the area managers at Waterloo, Clapham Junction, Woking, Basingstoke and Southampton, all of whom attended the headquarters meetings.

At the time, the local management organisations on the 'Southern' were somewhat different to the rest of British Rail in that station managers reported directly to the area managers who had limited resources and virtually no administrative backup. Some years later, this was reorganised to conform with the other regions. At Southampton, where I was assistant to the area manager, we did at least have a secretary and a clerical unit.

Earl Mountbatten was assassinated on 27 August 1979 while sailing off the coast of Northern Island. The area manager was on annual leave at the time which nearly presented a problem in getting access to the advance planning details, but eventually we obtained copies and could make sure the local arrangements at Romsey were well organised and that the station was 'spick and span'. A test train was run throughout on the Sunday prior to the actual date of the funeral and was totally successful. I spent most of that day accompanying the divisional manager at various briefing sessions at Romsey Abbey.

On Wednesday 5 September, following the conclusion of the State funeral service at Westminster Abbey, the arrangements became a private family matter. The train was treated accordingly. It departed Waterloo on time at 12.55, hauled by diesel electric locomotives 33027 and 33056. These bore no special embellishments and simply carried route indicator No. 94. The train itself looked quite ordinary, with six standard blue-and-grey liveried carriages and the maroon Royal Train Escort Vehicle 2906. The rear vehicle was a blue-and-grey passenger bogie brake van, which carried the earl's coffin.

Her Majesty the Queen, together with other members of the Royal Family and representatives of the European royal families and other dignitaries, travelled on the train, which left London on time and similarly arrived at Romsey at 2.30 p.m. As it glided to a stop, an eerie silence seemed to grip the whole station. The royal parties and mourners quietly alighted from the train. Suddenly, the silence was broken by a loud bang, rather like a gunshot. It was only the wind blowing shut a station door, but it must have brought an anxious moment for the security staff and marksmen covering the whole area.

The earl's coffin was removed from the brake van by the naval bearer party and the cortège solemnly made its way to the abbey. The departure brought our part in the occasion to its conclusion and, thankfully, it had been entirely satisfactory. Even so, it had been a sad day for the country as a whole and, in particular, for the area and Romsey station staff who had a close association with the earl. I felt a sense of pride that we had delivered all that was required of us on this historic occasion.

FOX AND BLOCKS

The last thing Geoff Body expected from his involvement with the Rocket 150 event was his discoveries in a peat bog

Apart from the journey to Warrington to join the Royal Air Force (and then on to West Kirby locked in a train in case I did not fancy eight weeks 'square-bashing'), I knew little about the North West and its railways. It was not until I had moved on from my railway years to a new field of writing and publishing railway books that I got to know it better. Despite a taste of road transport during a spell of running a national tank haulage company, railways were always my first love so I had kept in touch with the industry and my many friends within it. My small publishing company was already involved with the Western Region in the partnership production of books and postcards for railway publicity when the London Midland suggested we take on the task of preparing and publishing the official handbook for the celebration of the 150th anniversary of the Liverpool & Manchester Railway in 1980. This was to be a major event centred around a rolling stock display and parade at the location of the historic Rainhill Trials and I was honoured, excited and a little daunted by the task ahead of me.

My preparations had to be centred around the Liverpool area and its surviving L&M route to the old Liverpool Road station at Manchester. Fortunately, the then Liverpool divisional manager was Ken Dixon, to whom I had once been a supernumerary assistant in his days at Liverpool Street. He made me very welcome and deputed a member of his staff to bring me up to date on their preparations for

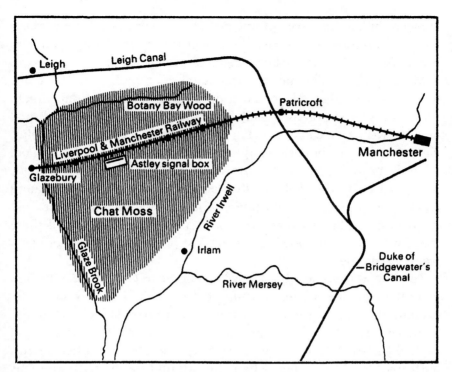

The railway crossing the peat bog.

the event and to act as my guide in the essential research I needed to do. Much of this entailed liaison with the Liverpool museum staff who had extensive archives and illustrations relating to the pioneer L&M line. I also needed to get a feel for its route and what remained of it. At that time it was still possible to see surviving evidence of the original works around places like Edge Hill, but I had also been excited by the saga of Chat Moss bog and wanted to go there as well.

In my preparatory reading, I was quite fascinated by the story of how George Stephenson and John Dixon took on the huge challenge of getting their railway across the formidable mass of peat bog which lay directly in its path between Patricroft and Glazebury. The so-called 'Blackpool Hole' at the heart of the boggy triangle was 35ft deep and the wet, soggy barrier itself stretched for some 3 miles across just where the railway needed to go. The engineers' answer was a raft on which to float the line, but it took a long while and a labour force of 200 men to find the right combination of materials to provide a stable base.

Stephenson later observed of one period in the process: 'After working for weeks and weeks ... there did not appear to be the least sign of our being able to raise the solid embankment a single inch.'

My Liverpool office mentor was obliging enough to take me out to see this legendary place, albeit on a rather dull, grey day which, somehow, proved exactly to match the nature of the dark and dismal area we were headed for. Leaving the car at the nearest access point, we tramped into the forbidding surroundings of Botany Bay Wood, squelching along the best route we could find between the pools, hummocks and the skeletal, stunted trees, all without foliage and creating a quite eerie atmosphere. There were no signs of life, just the opposite in fact for there, hanging from a branch of one of these trees, was what remained of a dead fox, presumably put there as a warning to others.

The line we were looking for seemed never to get any nearer until, painfully stubbing my toe, I stumbled on a stone and this, on closer examination was found to be a shaped and holed block. Our excitement was great! We had found one of the stone blocks which had carried the track of the original railway. There was another nearby, both discarded years ago when the original permanent way was first converted to a normal wooden sleeper base. These simple relics imparted a great sense of atmosphere and when the modern railway appeared just a short way further on, it looked so straight, well-maintained and modern that it was something of an anti-climax.

Fired by enthusiasm and with photographs duly taken, nothing would serve but that we unearthed our stone discovery, lugged it all the way back to the car and, tired, dirty and well-satisfied, we began the return journey that would eventually give our discovery into the care of Liverpool Museum.

The writing, publication and selling of the *Rocket 150 – Official Handbook* was a hectic, but rewarding follow-on. As was its photographic successor. The bonus for me lay rather in the further visits to locations associated with this marvellous original enterprise, the period of wandering around the gathering numbers of locomotives in Bold Colliery prior to the main Rainhill parade and then that day itself, when a glorious and fitting tribute was paid to the endeavour which began our railway industry.

WILLESDEN CARRIAGE SIDINGS

Demolished buffer stops, toilet and signal box put an end to Area Movements Inspector Chris Blackman's romantic weekend

On call duty at Willesden was alternate weeks, starting on Thursday evening, and did not involve Sunday as it was deemed that there were enough staff out on engineering work to respond to any problems. Saturday was also relatively free from calls as there were two middle turn inspectors who oversaw the station staff and were passed out on rules and regulations and thus able to attend to any emergency.

One weekend when I was on call my girlfriend came to stay. I perceived that the risks of being called out on the Saturday were minimal and on Sunday I was not scheduled for engineering work. However, these best-laid plans were wrecked at 9 a.m. on Saturday morning when Control rang to say that a locomotive had collided with the signal box at Willesden Carriage Shed South. Nobody was seriously hurt, but the signalling was completely disarranged. A taxi was on its way to take me to site. Ten minutes later my girlfriend had packed her bags and gone home to Guildford and I was sitting in a taxi wondering not only what scene would greet me at the site, but also whether I needed to look for another girlfriend.

The 350hp diesel shunting locomotive ('Jocko' in LM regional parlance) had been drawing some coaches southward along the side of the carriage shed towards a set of three ground-level shunting signals positioned one above the other. The driver misread the signals, thinking he was to proceed out past the signal box towards Euston, whereas the bottom signal, which was 'off', read towards the buffer stops, the signal box toilet and the box itself. The first two he destroyed completely and the third he knocked sideways by thirty degrees. It was a tribute to the LNWR engineers who built it that the structure not only brought the movement to a stand, but didn't collapse when the Jocko was extricated. The signalman was fortunately not in the little room at the time but, severely shocked, was sent home and

Willesden Carriage Shed South signal box pictured a couple of days after being struck by the Jocko, partly righted but still leaning. (Chris Blackman)

remained off sick for a week. Meanwhile I sent for a relief signalman, whilst the Signal & Telegraph staff disconnected all the points and signal levers. By mid-morning we had secured all the points and were on the move again with me as chief handsignalman.

Signal boxes are not the warmest of places, and with snow on the ground, some windows missing and doors not fitting up we were glad of the exercise to keep warm. The relief signalman who had joined me was the chairman of the signalmen's local departmental committee, named Sarras Ioannou, known to everyone as Johnny the Greek. At the first opportunity we slipped into the carriage shed to requisition some blankets and towels – fortuitously the shed's main role was servicing sleeping car trains – and were thus able to fill the bigger gaps in the signal box window and door frames. By the following day, when repairs to the head shunt had been completed, a mess coach was positioned on the head shunt and life was more comfortable in the dead period between train movements, particularly between 3 a.m. and 6 a.m.

Johnny and I, with two platelayers, spent the next week on twelve-hour nights, running round clipping points, signalling by hand, me checking routes properly set with no conflictions, and all of us retiring from time to time to stoke up the mess coach fire. The overtime was more than handy. Johnny, too, was always glad of overtime, and supplemented this by cleaning the platelayers out at poker each night!

Oh, and if you are wondering what became of the girlfriend, I am happy to say that we have now been married for over forty years. The overtime that week all helped to put down a deposit on a house a couple of years later.

WILLESDEN NEW LINE

The complexity and intense activity of the Willesden area gave Area Movements Inspector Chris Blackman quite a few interesting moments

Willesden New Line signal box was unusual. It was situated on and controlled the Dc (direct current) lines used by Bakerloo line trains as well as BR and accordingly the track was equipped with a fourth rail as well as a third rail. The box was normally closed and all signal telephones were switched to the next box ahead, Harrow No. 1 on the Down and Queens Park No. 3 on the Up. Access to the box was tricky, for although the box was just 20ft from the station island platform the Down line lay between the two. The walking route involved jumping off the platform on to the track and ensuring one didn't get taken by surprise by an approaching Bakerloo train. Health & safety inspectors would have had a fit, but luckily this was before 1974.

The box was only open for a few minutes a day for two principal functions. Most maintenance of the BR rolling stock on the line was carried out at Croxley depot in Watford, but certain repairs/overhaul were done at Willesden, and the access from the Dc lines to and from Willesden depot was controlled by New Line box. The regular weekday opening of the box was to deal with a train from Watford to Broad Street which arrived at Willesden at 08.33 and was booked to run via Hampstead Heath and Gospel Oak, taking the short connecting line immediately south of Willesden station up to Kensal Green Junction.

Although the Dc line from Euston to Primrose Hill was equipped by the LMS with signalling that was compatible with London

Underground practice, the connecting line was worked on the Absolute Block system with standard bells and instruments. So, for this unusual working, a signalman was rostered for a day shift at Willesden New line, but after the 08.33 had been dealt with he spent most of the day on other duties such as sweeping the platforms and checking tickets. Indeed, one old relief signalman connived with the roster clerk to cover the vacancy for months and thereby was better able to run his furniture removal business!

From time to time when the post was vacant and no relief signalman was available I would receive a telephone call in my office from the station supervisor that the 08.33 was approaching and no signalman was available. I would grab coat and hat, run down the road, turn right past the ticket collector, down the stairs two at a time to the platform to see the 08.33 coming to a stand in the Up platform, but be confronted by a Bakerloo approaching on the Down and completely blocking access to the box. As soon as the Bakerloo had gone on its way, and seemingly with all the passengers on the waiting 08.33 glaring at me, I would then jump off the platform across the Down track and rush up the steps into the signal box. There, in rapid succession, I had to throw the brown-and-white chevroned 'king' lever to normal, and, after sending 'Call Attention' of course, send the opening signal 5-5-5 to Kensal Green. Then it was, reset the facing points over, offer 3-1-2, get train accepted, pull signal off, bang in 2 for the 'Train Entering Section' signal, check track circuits clear, normalise the points, receive and acknowledge 2-1, send 7-5-5 to Kensal Green, pull off the king lever, wish Connie at Queens Park No. 3 good morning, fall down the box steps, look out for the next Bakerloo approaching and clamber up on to the platform. The reward was a cup of tea in the station inspector's office.

One of the two station inspectors was an ex-signalman so I passed him out to work the box in emergency and this substantially reduced the calls on my time. As a last resort when no one was available, the 08.33 went via Primrose Hill and a quite substantial number of passengers for stations to Gospel Oak had to alight and go to the high-level platform for the next train from Richmond.

UNFAMILIAR TERRITORY

**Some posts meant having to deal with a variety of
unfamiliar situations, nothing new in that for AMI
Chris Blackman at Willesden**

The Willesden area had thirty-four manual signal boxes plus the 'power box'. The latter, together with the power boxes at Euston and Watford, were the responsibility of the assistant chief divisional inspector, Jo Goodrum. Sadly Jo was in declining health, and within a matter of months he went on long-term sick leave, so the power boxes became the responsibility of the local area movements inspector. This meant I was in charge of over 100 signalmen with a range of nationalities, including West Indians from many different islands, some West Africans and three Cypriots (two Greek, one Turkish). On my first day I visited Gospel Oak No. 3 and met the first member of my staff. This signalman was a West Indian by the name of Neville White, and the news that White had met Blackman caused some amusement along the line.

Kew East Junction, a signal box at one end of the Willesden area and an eerie place on a moonlit night with a graveyard just behind the trees. (Chris Blackman)

In 1970 Willesden absorbed the Kensington area and thus the seven signal boxes on the West London line came within my on-call area. The first box down the line, fringing with Mitre Bridge, was North Pole Junction. It was difficult to fill vacancies at this box as many of the trainee signalmen in the divisional training school were of West African or West Indian origin and were convinced that North Pole was a very cold place to be and, moreover, it looked towards Wormwood Scrubs prison nearby. The very first week after I took 'on call' for the West London I was called out at midnight to North Pole signal box where the BT (British Transport) police had reason to interview the night turn signalman urgently. Indeed, so urgently that as soon as I arrived they arrested him on a charge of aiding and abetting the theft of mailbags. For this he and his mate were later convicted and spent the next year or so looking out from the Scrubs at the signal box!

Meanwhile I set about working the box for the rest of the night shift. As well as being cold, the box was gas lit but, with the assistance of my Bardic hand lamp, I signed on, checked the equipment and looked back through a few pages of entries in the Train Register. Then the telephone rang and I answered it saying 'North Pole', to be informed, '3-1-1 on the Down'. In response I gave my name and rank and enquired stiffly who was speaking at the other end and why he was not offering the train on the block bells. He answered: 'This is Viaduct junction and there's a block failure.'

Bearing in mind that I had looked back through the Train Register, I responded: 'Since when?'

The reply was: 'A couple of weeks ago.'

On going back several pages – and previous to the Kensington inspector's most recent visit – there was indeed an entry to that effect. I accepted the train and asked its identity to establish that it was for the GW main line. The next hurdle was to offer trains to the latter's Old Oak power box which, from examination of the equipment on the blockshelf, appeared to be by inputting the train headcode.

This I did ... Nothing happened ... I tried again ... No response ... I lifted the handset to speak to the power box ... Still no response.

I looked around with my Bardic and found a standard telephone with a dial and, what luck, a list of useful telephone numbers on the wall, including that of the 'OO PSB'. This time the phone was answered immediately and I was advised that the headcode dialling equipment had not worked for some years, but furthermore that OO was happy to accept the parcels train that was now approaching my Home signal. Relieved that I now seemed to be getting somewhere, I set the road towards the GWML (GW main line) and pulled the signal lever. Or tried to. With my Bardic in one hand I first checked that the road was set – confirmed; checked secondly that I had the release from OO box – yes; checked next for any electric locks on the block shelf above the lever – nothing. I started sweating! I remembered Corporal Jones's advice, 'Don't panic', so carefully rechecked everything, but all appeared correctly set. Then – ah, what's this? A knob in the semi-darkness protruding out halfway down the signal lever? Never seen anything like this before, I thought, but hey-ho, I have never worked a GW frame before, so let's see what it does. I tried depressing it, but met resistance. Lifting the knob proved more successful, and there was a satisfying click as the electric lock released. I pulled the lever over and with a sigh of relief watched the parcels train rumble past, then checked the tail lamp, reset the road, gave 'Train Out of Section' to Viaduct, and completed the entries in the register before filling the kettle. The rest of the shift was uneventful, with normal working to Mitre Bridge and Regulation 25(a)(iii) to Viaduct. Nothing else passed on the connection to the Old Oak power box, and in the cold light of dawn I handed over to the early turn signalman, signed the register, and went home in a taxi kindly provided by Control.

During the journey home I reflected on the potential hazards of having to work a signal box in near darkness and without previously visiting it. I also pondered briefly whether I would have rather continued with academic studies and become a university lecturer, but concluded without hesitation that railways were much more fun! And on that note I slept soundly.

DOUBLE DERAILMENT

Either the Crawley stationmaster knew something or Peter Thomas was unlucky in timing

In the 1950s I was sent to Crawley to cover the stationmaster's leave. Crawley New Town was under construction at the time, but the remains of the original town were still discernible. An additional train from Brighton ran to Crawley each day conveying construction workers and there was an extreme shortage of labour in the area. I should have had six porters, but there were only two. I had arranged lodgings near to the signal box, but went home on nights when not on call.

Engineering works were planned for the approaching weekend which would block the Up line between Faygate and Crawley, with single-line working (SLW) over the Down line between those two points. Harry Bennet, the stationmaster at Three Bridges, came down to help in preparing the single-line forms.

All was ready, so on the Saturday I went for lunch at the Horsham canteen. On my way back to the station I heard that several wagons of the 10.58 Chichester to Norwood had been derailed between Faygate and Crawley. The train I was on was stopped at Littlehaven Halt as the line was blocked. What a bad start!

I telephoned the booking clerk at Crawley and arranged for him to send a taxi for me. I would have to put in SLW between the two places, having established that the Down line was clear. One of the porters was to be the pilotman while the other remained at Crawley to direct passengers to the Down platform which would deal with trains in both directions. Calling Brighton Loco to order the breakdown crane would have meant going via Redhill and Brighton switchboards on a primitive system, so I asked Redhill Control to do it for me. The local permanent way staff clipped the points where necessary.

The wayward wagons were re-railed and attended to by the Carriage & Wagon staff, who made them fit to be moved to Crawley at walking pace. When they eventually arrived, they were to be set back into the yard but – another catastrophe – they derailed again, this time blocking the Up line to Three Bridges. There was nothing for it but to extend the SLW further. At this stage something better happened when my landlady arrived with some freshly made ham sandwiches, saying she thought I would be hungry and unable to get in for tea. I was truly grateful.

That was more than enough for the Saturday. On the Sunday morning Basil Bushell, the assistant district traffic superintendent, came to inspect the work planned. Tom Mann, the area inspector, came across to me and demanded to know why I did not have a handsignalman at the Down Home signal as the rules required. Fortunately all Down trains were running under caution from Three Bridges to Crawley so his criticism was a bit harsh.

The rest of the day went off well and I went home feeling a bit in need of some R&R (rest and relaxation). At the joint inquiry I was not criticised and was duly thankful. On reflection, I thought that George Jary, the stationmaster I was relieving, might have chosen a better time for his annual leave!

THUNDERSLEY

One locomotive came to epitomise an era on the small but important LT&S lines, as Theo Steel reveals in his account of its role as the star of the centenary celebrations

The railway in question was the London, Tilbury & Southend (LT&S) line and the locomotive so often associated with it was the 4-4-2 tank *Thundersley*. The railway itself, essentially two routes from Fenchurch Street to Shoeburyness via Upminster and a loop down to Tilbury, had been conceived to convey Londoners to the latter point to catch the ferry across to pleasure gardens at Rosherville, near Gravesend. It came to be vastly more than that with a huge commuter activity and, in later years, considerable freight carryings.

For much of its life, LT&S trains were worked by 4-4-2 tank engines, all named after places they served. *Thundersley* itself was one of the last four Whitelegg-designed engines, built at the Robert Stephenson works in 1909, although there were further examples built by the LMS

In splendid condition, LT&S No. 80 *Thundersley* heads an RC&TS special run as part of the 1956 centenary celebrations of the line. (Alan Sprod)

in the late 1920s. The design was a development of the staple LTS power, which went back to No. 1 *Southend* built by Sharp Stewart in 1880. *Thundersley* was renamed *Southend-on-Sea* and exhibited in the 1909 Imperial International Exhibition at White City shortly after it was built, where it won a gold medal. It was also decorated to celebrate the 1912 coronation of King George V. The locomotive spent most of its career on the LTS, in frontline service until the mid-1930s when the 2-6-4 Stanier 3-cylinder tanks arrived and was more or less surplus by the time the 80,000 Riddles tanks appeared in force in the 1950s.

The 1956 centenary of the LTS was celebrated in some considerable style as I was reminded when Alan Sprod circulated some of his pictures. There was an exhibition on Platforms 5 and 6 at Southend Central for the week ending 3 March. You could see No. 27002, a Manchester–Sheffield passenger electric that later ran in Holland, No. 80080 one of the recently arrived Riddles tanks, Britannia No. 70038 *Robin Hood*, and the record-breaking *Mallard* on the now removed platform 6. There was also a Class 08 shunter. To represent the modern era, one of the all-but-new Class 307 units introduced with the electrification of the Southend Victoria line the previous month was also present, and the exhibition was complemented by an indoor fair in the foyer of the then Odeon cinema in the high street.

The centenary event culminated with a 'special' train hauled by *Thundersley* and including a veteran LTS coach as well as coaches from the pre-war prestige service which ran non-stop from Westcliff-on-Sea to Fenchurch Street in fifty minutes in the morning and back in the evening. The special traversed the original route via Tilbury and into Liverpool Street via Forest Gate. Period dress was worn by the participants.

To mark the occasion *Thundersley* was immaculate in green with claret lining, I recall, and followed up by working an RCTS special. It was then set aside successively in the Derby Works round house and Hellifield before being moved to Bressingham, where it was put on show as part of the National Collection. The LTS coach fared less well and was, sadly, cut up at Stratford in around 1960.

The 1956 event was neither the first nor the last such celebration. A Royal Scot locomotive was exhibited at Southend Central in 1935 following conversations when the LMS Board attended the opening of Leigh-on-Sea station. Not to be outdone, the LNER countered with an exhibition celebrating fifty years of the Southend Victoria line in 1938 at that station, and including the record-breaking *Mallard*. Since then a HST (High Speed Train) was famously run from Southend Central to Liverpool Street and back in February 1981, thanks to co-operation between then divisional managers Bill Parker and Gordon Pettit, and 107mph was allegedly reached passing Becontree. In 1988 Southend Victoria hosted a visit by the preserved N7 suburban tank engine on the centenary of that route and in 2006 a dinner train was run on the LTS. There have been steam specials since, including a visit of *Tornado* as recently as December 2012, but nothing before or since has quite rivalled the March 1956 festival which attracted over 50,000 visitors I understand – including myself as a 7 year old!

TRACK SUBSIDENCE

Maintaining the permanent way on a heavily used line above a coalfield is no easy matter, as Jim Dorward reveals

It is Monday, 9 May 1960. I am with one of the permanent way engineers from the Perth District Engineer's office. We have had to make an unexpected journey by road to Thornton Junction on the Edinburgh to Dundee section of the East Coast Main Line. The local permanent way inspector has telephoned to say that the Up road has gone down by about 6in, which means that he is having to deal with a sudden case of track subsidence. This is a common occurrence in this area as it is in the Fife coalfield and directly above old and new coal workings. In fact, we know almost exactly where the coal has been extracted, as BR's mining engineer in Glasgow regularly provides the district engineer with drawings showing exactly where the NCB plans to work.

To ease maintenance, the track is on ash instead of stone ballast and a long 15mph speed restriction is in place on both the Down and Up lines. It is very easy to see where this latest problem has happened. With some concern, we watch a long coal train pass slowly over the subsidence. We see the 16-ton mineral wagons 'free wheel' into the dip and then shudder violently as the slack in the couplings is taken up when they start to be pulled out. It is reassuring to see the coupled driving wheels of the ex WD 2-8-0 steam engine managing to deal with the rollercoaster track.

The local permanent way gang is in attendance to deal with any repacked sleepers that suddenly subside unevenly under the weight of the trains, thereby creating an excessive twist in the track that could easily cause a derailment. They are used to this firefighting type of track maintenance, which has to be carried out in the short time interval between trains. Dealing with track geometry seriously affected by ongoing mining subsidence reminds us of the basic requirement to keep the rails in contact with the wheels, as it is all too easy in this situation for a fault to develop that causes a wheel to end up with fresh air between it and the rail.

Although we are having difficulty keeping coal wagons on the track, we know that the mechanical engineers are also having trouble keeping that coal in the wagons! This is because the wagon retarders just ahead of the hump in the new Thornton marshalling yard are still stopping wagons instead of slowing them down, causing vast amounts of coal to be catapulted on to the track!

We make a survey of the subsidence area using a Dumpy Level. Tomorrow, back at the office, we will use the readings to design a new gradient profile and work out the track lifts that will need to be carried out next Sunday when the lines will be blocked and we can have access.

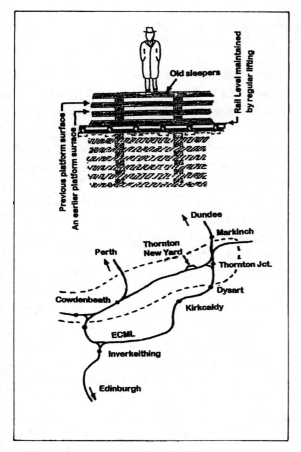

The coalfield area around Thornton made the local railway lines liable to subsidence. (Jim Dorward)

Before leaving Thornton, we check platform heights. When subsidence occurs the platforms are allowed to sink but, of course, the track has to be lifted up to the correct level. This means that every few years, another layer of old sleepers has to be laid on the platforms to provide the correct height difference between platform and trains. Consequently, the amount of platform now 'buried' underground is considerable!

The permanent way inspector and his men are living with a never-ending problem. The effort required to keep the busy East Coast Main Line in this area fit for 15mph running is way beyond the gentle manicuring that keeps the track on the lightly used West Coast Main Line between Perth and Kinnaber Junction (via Forfar) in perfect condition. It seems unfair that the PWI (permanent way inspector) at Thornton and his gangs are never going to win the Best Kept Length Competition!

SHOW AND TELL

The TOPS system gave BR total oversight of rolling stock and train movement information for the first time. Peter Spedding had a hand in its beginnings

In September 1971 I was appointed coding assistant to the newly formed Total Operations Processing System (TOPS) team and moved to Blandford House, which was to be the home of the project.

My position had still to be defined so I did a variety of jobs including an investigation into how the timetable was to be represented in the system. It was all new and full of complications for at this stage there was no computer so our work had to be theoretical.

Early in 1972 the IBM mainframe computer was installed – nothing like our present generation of machines – and, shortly afterwards, we received the version of the TOPS currently running on the Southern Pacific Railroad (SPR) in the USA. This purely American system was 'supported' by no less than five thick volumes of field procedures. Its geography was Southern Pacific and the locomotives and rolling stock were all 'off line', i.e. not linked to any location or with any load or destination information. All rather confusing!

Despite these daunting factors it was decided that there must be 'Show and Tell' demonstrations, both for gaining experience and to give people outside the project a broad appreciation of what the system was all about. I was given the job of staging this, with the help of Nick DiCroce, one of the SPR people over here.

The first job was reading the relevant field procedures to find out how to report working events to the system and this immediately raised the problem of understanding the US terminology – what was a gondola, head end power etc. Geography was another problem, as the place names and their relationship to one another had little meaning to us. Inevitably, stations like Suisan Fairfield got converted to Susan Fairfield in our interpretation.

We selected a portion of the SP system that would make a reasonable, but not too complicated demonstration. Train schedules were loaded in together with several trains of thirty or forty wagons (or 'cars', in American parlance), their destinations and loads, and locomotives were allocated.

After much trial and error and the laborious task of punching thousands of the eighty-column cards to load all this information on to the computer, we eventually produced a workable system. For over a year this performed the vital function of demonstrating the possibilities of TOPS to officers from all over BR. A rewarding result, but not without its birth pains!

THE FINANCE MANAGER

The finance manager's task was difficult and not always popular, but could achieve the sort of worthwhile results revealed by Nick Wood

In late 1982 I was fortunate enough to be appointed finance manager (operations) at Waterloo. My geographical knowledge of the Southern Region (SR) was very sketchy, having spent the previous twenty-four years on other regions. Two weeks into the new job I arrived at work to be informed that the chief operating manager, Alec Bath, wished to see me to discuss the budget and I was to join him on the 09.00 from London Bridge to Brighton. 'How do I get to London Bridge?' was my panicky response, but my assistant piloted me over to Waterloo East, put me on a train and reminded me that the next stop was London Bridge, and that I should not forget to get out! All went well fortunately, but for a time after that I always carried a detailed map of the Southern Region and consulted this surreptitiously to make sure I knew what others were talking about.

After the divisions were closed, the SR operating budget embraced the costs of twenty-two areas and headquarters, mostly for some 20,000 staff. At one unforgettable budget review meeting not all went too well. As we walked to it, the Chief Operating Manager asked me, 'How much can we give away?'

'A quarter of a million,' I said. 'Half a million if they really twist your arm, but absolutely no more.'

So there we were, the general manager and all the regional chief officers and their finance managers. After some discussion the GM remarked bluntly that our budget was unsustainable and had to be cut by £2 million. Without thinking, I blurted out, 'B***dy hell, we can't do that!' The GM looked at me and commented calmly that that was how it had to be, while my boss whispered to me, 'If you are going to make comments like that, I should keep your voice down.' We had to accept the drastic cut and all its consequences in terms of closed booking offices, cancelled trains, reduced cleaning and all the public complaints. Fortunately, the overall BR financial position improved as the year went on, allowing us to mitigate some of the cuts we had made.

The area reviews which preceded these regional meetings could be tough going. I recall one unproductive review with David Jones at Orpington. After three hours of discussion, all we had achieved was the reduction of one post. The area manager knew every blade of grass on his patch and could justify every post in his organisation. Of course, that was how it should be. All the same it was very frustrating for us!

With the introduction of sectorisation on BR in 1986 all the infrastructure was divided between the new 'Businesses'. Track renewals were a capital item and, as such, were funded separately from the normal day-to-day income and expenditure. Each business was given a capital figure by the BRB and it was up to the managing director to allocate this between his divisions. In Network South East, we had ten of these and their bids for funds always came to more than the total available.

In one year in particular West Anglia Great Northern (WAGN), of which I was financial controller, accepted a reduced budget, but sought an assurance that our bid the following year would receive more sympathy. In due course, I made myself a thorough nuisance to the InterCity Civil Engineer at Peterborough, who was contracted to undertake Slow Line renewals on the GN main line, and to our own civil engineer David Watson, who looked after the Hertford Loop and the Cambridge main line.

Every scheme they put forward was subjected to, 'What are the implications of not doing it? Why does it cost so much? Can you increase the line speed? What reductions in track maintenance costs can we expect?' And so on.

As a result of all this we went to the meeting with the managing director with a detailed list of what we wanted and why, and took David along to mitigate his exasperation with the grilling he had received from me. In the event, we got most of what we wanted, and David's comment after the meeting was, 'I never believed it would be like that; now I know why all those questions were asked!'

Controlling engineering expenditure was never easy, especially as our esteemed infrastructure manager, Chris Eastman, had assured me on one occasion, 'I will squander your money wisely!'

In my organisation I had a clerical officer whose duty it was to monitor and pay all utility company invoices, which involved checking an awful lot of meters. He was very good at it too, and saved WAGN a lot of money by challenging the level of charges and, in some cases, our responsibility to pay. One notable example was the water at Ashwell, on the Hitchin–Cambridge line. He could not understand why the usage was so high. On investigation we found that we were paying for the water to the former railway cottages near the station. Apparently this had been going on for years. He prevailed upon the water company to install a separate meter for the cottages and came to an arrangement with the occupiers for recompense for their past free water.

We found Railtrack difficult to deal with, and I had one or two 'run ins' with them. In common with all the commuter franchises we were a cash business, even better than supermarkets because the cash from season tickets gave us a surplus which we could lend short term to earn interest.

Every four weeks WAGN paid Railtrack around £2 million for track access. In the run-up to Easter I received a rather peremptory fax from their finance manager saying that as normal banking would not be available on Good Friday, we *must* pay them by noon on Thursday. Not likely, I thought, we would lose interest on that money, so I replied that we would pay as soon as the banks reopened on the Tuesday after the holiday. Oh dear; I was threatened with all sorts of dire consequences. All to no avail, they had to wait for their money. To their further discomfort I also contacted my colleagues in the other three Prism franchises and told them what I was doing, and they all followed suit!

THE DENTON BRANCH

Bryan Stone tells of another branch line, ironstone and an obstructive engine

This little trip was during New Year leave in 1961, while I was still on the Longmoor Military Railway and looking forward to starting with BR. A personal invitation took me to Belvoir, a few miles from our family home near Nottingham, a signal box on the old 'Ambergate', more properly known as the GN (Great Northern) Nottingham–Grantham line. The plan was to join the driver, a Colwick man, on the footplate of J39 No. 64804, to go up a curious branch which now, like the signal box, the engine and the reason for the line itself, has disappeared as if all had never been.

The Duke of Rutland at Belvoir Castle knew that he had iron ore under his pastures. It was everywhere, along a ridge extending at least to Holwell near Melton Mowbray, and was tapped from all sides by competing railways. The GN's Denton Branch was an old one, started in 1883 and extended as the mines grew. Stewarts & Lloyds and Stanton Ironworks found the ore suitable, and mines were dug, and a whole cat's cradle of standard- and narrow-gauge mineral lines fed from the quarries into the GN's, and now BR's, 5¾-mile single-line branch south-east from Belvoir to Denton. A mile of this was on the towpath of the Grantham Canal, which the GNR had bought out; it was all lightly laid, and other bits were quite steeply graded. It was signalled by train staff, controlled by Belvoir, though there was rarely more than one engine up the branch.

Unlike the much busier branch from Highdyke, which the Working Timetable dismissed with just 'worked as required', the Denton line had its own timetable, with scheduled trips. My 1959 Lincoln area Freight Train WTT, which covers the lines from Colwick to the east, shows three Class J through freights Denton to Colwick (for Stanton Ironworks), and three trips from Denton down to Belvoir, on weekdays. These might end up as a Frodingham load from Belvoir, for which no booked path was shown, but one left during my visit.

On my day, No. 64804 was waiting, tender-first, to take the 9.40 a.m. trip, some twenty-five empty iron-ore tipplers, up the branch to Harlaxton and Denton, arriving at 10.25 a.m. It would then collect loaded ore tipplers, to leave at 12.12 p.m. as a Class J working from Belvoir Junction to Colwick, taking fifty minutes for the 17-mile haul. The loads were prepared by the mines and in some cases were hauled in several miles on private tramways by industrial locomotives.

The track was rough, the riding brutal, the grade severe – 1 in 57 near Woolsthorpe. I was enthralled by the working on this low-speed see-saw. But once up at Denton, where end-on connections and

Running tender first, No. 64804 heads a train of empties on the climb up the bank to Woolsthorpe on the Denton branch. (Bryan Stone)

The driver of No. 64804 struggles with the consequences of the worn out valve gear on his locomotive. (Bryan Stone)

a ground frame gave access to the private lines, I and the crew were in for another surprise, for which my Longmoor experience had not prepared me. When the driver reversed No. 64804, before working the exchange sidings at Denton, and to shunt the yard, the worn-out valve gear gave up. There was a woolly puff one way, a shuddering stop, pitching us across the footplate, another puff the other way, and another sudden stop. I knew even then that this could break couplings and provoke runaways, as the wagons, all un-braked, clanged about on their three-link couplings. Brake on hard, the regulator – on this engine the Gresley vertical pull-out lever – slammed shut, and the driver tried reversing again. No response. Were we stuck? He let her roll half a turn on the grade, she reversed herself, and soon we had our train together and were off downhill to Belvoir, brakes pinned down, with a heavy load. I learned some new expressions which together suggested that J39s, and No. 64804 in particular, were out of favour, but it was when they were already being rapidly withdrawn. I never rode one again, but it had been an instructive morning.

I never got up to Denton again. The line closed in 1966, but opened for a year in 1977 before total abandonment. Today, where railwaymen toiled for years to keep things going, virtually everything has gone.

RED NOSE DAY

An innocent incident could have spoiled an important David Crathorn relationship at Landor Street Customs Shed

In the 1960s a number of ways were developed to improve the rail movement and security of goods, especially those in the international trade. The Freightliner container replaced the old, widely used A and B type railway containers. Shipping companies produced the ISO standard containers which were much stronger and had standard dimensions and lifting pockets. It was felt necessary to keep containers sealed, but the customs officers at the ports wanted containers opened for their inspection.

This situation led BR to seek inland customs clearance at various major inland centres. One of these, unsurprisingly, was Birmingham

– 'the city of 1,000 trades' – which exported many different manu-
factured items. The LMR (London Midland Region) Metal Shed, at
the bottom end of Lawley Street Freight Depot, was available. It was
of good size, with a good roof, and it had a separate gate leading to
Landor Street. Even better, it had a concrete deck with a rail siding
along one edge and lorry backing-up points on the opposite side. There
were brick offices across the end. It was ideal as a customs shed.

As traffic grew I was appointed as assistant area manager at Aston,
in charge of the full load traffic at Lawley Street and the adjacent
customs depot. It was an interesting position, involving a variety of
wagon load movements, quite a few needing cartage, and a considerable road collection and delivery workload. I took a close interest in
the work, including shunting, and the staff took pride in their job.

Sadly, it was decided to close the Lawley Street depot and convert it
into a Freightliner terminal.

Freightliners Limited did not want the customs shed activity so I was
appointed as its inland port manager, including two sidings and a road-
way alongside.

There followed a steady increase in customs traffic, both import and
export. The imports were kept in a large steel cage on the deck, and only
released after the customs officer had signed them 'out of charge'. Our
checker, Fred Pugh, who had been displaced from the ex-GWR Hockley
goods depot, used to keep everything in the import cage in good order,
the other staff members working around the site as required. After
clearance inland, containers stayed sealed through to destination.

Because we were so busy, the LMR decided to build another customs depot nearby and designed specifically for containers. This was
sited on the former cattle depot at Banbury Street. With the original
access route having been taken out of use, there was no access from
Banbury Street itself and so the new depot was connected to and called
Montague Street International Container Depot.

On reflection, I could have been elsewhere if I had fancied a bit of
quiet. But life was too busy for that and, even in the evenings, I could be
out with the shipping men or road hauliers when I sometimes picked
up some new traffic.

After a while, my wife said that she would like to see where I worked.
She drove over from our home in Wolverhampton one day, bringing
with her our 18-month-old son. We had coffee together and I showed

her Montague Street, but at that moment not much was happening there so we drove to the customs shed, spent a while in the office and then went through to the main shed. It was busy, and we had to stand aside while a forklift truck carried a big case past. We walked on, chatted with some of the staff and saw Fred busy with his paperwork.

Suddenly, a man appeared from behind a stack of cases and, seeing me, strode up to us. He was our customs officer. I began to introduce my wife and son when, suddenly, the little boy reached out and grabbed the ample nose of the customs man. Fred and the other staff let out gasps of horror. The customs man was one to be revered, and there he was 'under attack'!

I am very, very glad that our particular customs officer was extremely understanding and not, apparently, injured. We continued our walkabout and the incident had no repercussions, but I shall not forget it. My son is now 45, running his own inn and brewing some excellent bitter, and has no recollection of his infant assault on a quite important official.

'GET RID OF IT'

To Cedric Spiller fell the sad task of demolishing the prestige wine operation of British Transport Hotels

During 1981 I was appointed to head up the Wines Division of British Transport Hotels (BTH), almost certainly because I knew nothing about wine, but did have a lot of experience in logistics and supply chain management. The division was in a mess with vast stocks and an administrative system that was a nightmare.

At a point around 1983/84 I was summoned to the boardroom at St Pancras Chambers where the great and the good were assembled, including a number of individuals who knew nothing about railway operations and asked – if that is the right word – what was the value of the stock. In response to such naïve arrogance (things were pretty feudal at that period) I enquired of them if they wanted a value 'in bond' or 'duty paid'. The upshot was £5.6 million duty paid. 'Oh dear,' they muttered. 'As much as that!'

The former BTH hotel at Manchester, an impressive 500-bedroom design by the Midland Railway's architect Charles Trubshaw and opened in 1903.

It then transpired that a certain high governmental figure was very annoyed to find out that this clapped out railway had bottling plants, wine cellars, wine shops, and vast on-train and station catering operations. Oh, and somewhere along the line were a number of hotels – God forbid, with golf courses!

Then came the somewhat Churchillian instruction: 'Get rid of it.'

And so it came to pass that I did. Firstly, and most importantly, was the need to protect the officers' and management messes! So a lorry load of crates of Chablis, Hautes-Côtes de Beaune, Corton and Pouilly-Fuissé were despatched to the St Pancras kitchens. Next came the valuation of the stock by a well-known London auctioneer. Then the appointment of an agent. Then it got messy!

First to go was the Derby cellars and bottling plant. All staff on the scrapheap, the equipment to the scrap merchant (apart from some important artefacts quietly disposed of to various preservation centres and heritage bodies) and the wine to the new agent in London.

Secondly came the clear-out of the East London cellars, stock to north-west London, fittings to the East End scrap boys (my, they were a dodgy lot!), more staff on the scrapheap and the premises turned over to become a city slickers' car park.

Then the forty-nine staff associated with the Wine Club and the headquarters administration. As the hotels were going as well, the third floor of St Pancras Chambers was officially labelled the 'Gissus a Job Centre'. With an appalling level of poor staff consultation and reneging on agreements, the next three months were punctuated by scenes of grown men and women crying, throwing wobblies and attending the long sequence of 'farewell booze-ups' – or should I say 'wine-ups'!

One aspect that also caused a near riot was the retrieval of wine stocks from those BTH hotels that were being transferred to the private sector. Many had vast quantities reserved for various Masonic events and special occasions involving politicians and film stars. The lengths that some managers went to in order to hide their wares were astonishing and ingenious. We got most if it though.

With Travellers Fare going into the private sector (their wine stocks were small and pure mass-produced plonk) that was the end of a long tradition that had seen the railway hotels operation at the very pinnacle of wine supply in the UK. Most of the bonded claret, including Petrus and Lafite, went to the USA or the Far East for a song.

As for me, I was on the BTH scrapheap too, turning up every day to an empty office in order to do the *Guardian* cryptic crossword before going home. Then a telephone call one morning from a long lamented chief officer at BRB HQ enquired: 'Are you the silly bugger sitting doing crosswords, if so get your **** up here now.'

End of demolition activity, new challenges beckoned.

Anyone who has ever been involved in this sort of destruction of a great operation, just for political reasons, will understand that the human price is enormous. At the same time others often make a fortune from the process without overmuch thought for the people involved.

And anyone who remembers *The Boys from the Blackstuff* will understand what it is to have to say 'Gissus a Job'.

CARDIFF FREIGHT 1967–71

Two major new activities were added to the traditional South Wales coal and steel freight business while David Jagoe was at Cardiff

With seven steelworks and several deepmine and opencast collieries in South Wales, the Cardiff Division of the Western Region relied heavily for revenue on steel and coal transport, both within and outside the area. Despite the limited range of commodities, further restricted by shortage of rolling stock capable of accommodating the full range of steel products, the division, nevertheless, more than held its own in terms of freight volume and revenue by comparison with other BR divisions. The only other interesting movements of significance were daily services for fresh fish from Milford Haven and fresh milk in tanks from Whitland.

Coal was conveyed in trainloads of 16-ton mineral wagons with sections being made up in Severn Tunnel Junction Yard to the domestic markets, mainly in the London and Home Counties. The crushed and washed coal, a proportion recovered from the old colliery waste tips, was conveyed in trainloads of bottom-door discharge 'Merry-Go-Round' (MGR) wagons (so called because cargo could be loaded and unloaded whilst moving) to the power stations, mainly at Didcot and Aberthaw. There were also local movements of coking coal for the two main steelworks with blast furnaces at Newport and Port Talbot. Apart from securing a new contract to convey 1.1 million tonnes of iron ore from Newport Docks to the steelworks at Ebbw Vale, any growth in tonnage was largely organic and relied upon increased demand for output of the two major industries.

The arrival of Freightliner in 1968 had a significant effect by opening up new freight marketing opportunities. The Hon. Barbara Castle, then Minister for Transport, cut the tape at the new Pengam terminal at Cardiff. Despite the opposition from the Freightliner management at the Board, local management insisted in providing a small fleet of prime movers only, and selling the service to the major road hauliers in South Wales, on the grounds that they already had much of the potential business, had the vehicles, and were familiar with the despatch and delivery processes. On the strength of the argument that it would be to BR's advantage to have the hauliers as customers and partners rather than as competitors and, inevitably, as winners, the board conceded the point. A similar philosophy was applied to the Swansea terminal a year later.

At the same time, Freightliner sets were placed into the loading docks at each of the three major rolling mills, so opening up the opportunity to compete for the whole range of steel products, including the vulnerable-to-handling cold rolled steel, both in coil and sheet form. A salesman visited each mill daily to identify and secure every piece that was labelled and destined for the London and Home Counties and ensure that they were all loaded to the service. Thus the 'Steelliner' was born, with its own specialised terminal in London at Park Royal. Subsequently services were developed to other destinations, in particular one to Sheffield which became almost exclusively a Ross Transport service, very largely loaded by the road haulier in both directions.

The other major freight opportunity arose when the contractors constructing the M5 motorway section across the Somerset Levels discovered that the conventional method of placing heavy material to form the embankment foundations didn't apply in Somerset. The heavy boulders and rocks kept sinking into the marshy ground overnight!

So the boffins at the Central Electricity Generating Board came up with a solution, 'fly-ash': the waste material at power stations. When wet this material forms a very strong, rigid and durable, yet extremely lightweight, structure. The resultant opportunity to move the enormous tips of fly-ash from the power stations in South Wales was duly seized, with the co-operation of the train crews at Newport depot, helped by a couple of good parties at the local staff association premises. Five sets of MGR wagons 'stolen' from the national coal business were used: one set loading, one discharging, one en route, one returning empty and one set in preventative maintenance. Two simple and temporary discharge facilities were constructed by the BR Bristol engineers on temporary running loops off the main line near Highbridge, ensuring a slick and extremely effective seven-days-a-week continuous operation. Everyone was a winner: the CEGB was able to dispose a large quantity of its waste material at a price, the contractors were dug out of the 'mire', and BR won an effective and extremely profitable contract.

A TALE OF TWO
BRANCHES

'I was just looking round which, in our earliest years, we were encouraged to do,' reasons Bryan Stone

I had in the Doncaster Division a couple of branch line experiences which, within a very short time, would be lost forever. One was on our doorstep. About three-quarters of a mile by road from Gresley House beside Doncaster station was a small goods yard. By rail it was a long way, because it could only be reached via Hexthorpe, on the Great Central line to Rotherham, and reversing there.

A signal box called 'Doncaster Junction' might, you would think, be in the middle of things at Doncaster. Not so; although several pre-grouping railways had served Doncaster station and its yards, the Hull & Barnsley, whose box it was, did not. Now, the H&B, built to frighten the benevolently despotic monopolist North Eastern Railway at Hull, was a clear case of 'last in, first out', and much of it was already derelict by 1964. Not opened until May 1916, the historian C.T. Goode started his description with: 'The most remarkable thing about this line [the Aire to Braithwell branch] was that it was built at all.'

Starting from Aire Junction on the H&B main line from Hull, it reached nearly due south some 21 miles, mostly through open country, with a strategic scissors junction at Sprotborough Junction on the Doncaster Avoiding Line as it passed west of the town. Then, 1 mile 1,242yd north of this, and south of Bullcroft Colliery, was Doncaster Junction, and at the end of a ¾-mile branch was Doncaster York Road.

On a February day in 1964 I visited York Road, attracted by signs of life, steam and smoke in the winter morning. It was a terminus, blocked from going nearer to Doncaster by the embankment of the Avoiding Line towards Barnby Dun, and in a triangular site by a major road junction. There was an island platform, to which the H&B perhaps hoped

K1 locomotive 62066, one of the last LNER classes to survive, shunts York Road Yard at Doncaster. The platform behind was never used. (Bryan Stone)

one day to run a Hull–Doncaster local service, but which no passenger trains had ever used, also the stationmaster's house (let, but not to a stationmaster), the petrol store siding and the Doncaster Co-operative Dairy siding. Some wagons of scrap stood at one side.

K1 Class locomotive No. 62066, recently 'cascaded' to Doncaster shed as withdrawals of steam raced ahead, was butting wagons up and down. A friendly shout from the guard, who was also the shunter, made me welcome, and I was 'inspecting the working', not really too demanding. A few years before, the engine would have been the Sprotborough Junction banking pilot, which at mid-morning went to Hexthorpe and Doncaster to fetch the York Road traffic, returning afterwards to its post. That had all gone, and Sprotborough Junction was now quiet. Today's activity was a trip by Control orders from Doncaster where my notes say that the Down Mineral Yard would have set out the increasingly rare wagons for York Road.

The 1916 H&B and GC (Great Central) joint line south of Sprotborough Junction was now closed south to Braithwell. The Doncaster Avoiding Line from Hexthorpe is, I believe, still there.

The block coal loads for Thorpe Marsh, from South Yorkshire, about which I wrote in an earlier volume, went along the H&B to Bullcroft and into the power station siding; the line north of there was already abandoned. Thorpe Marsh traffic justified that line until closure in the 1990s, but I had left in 1968, and York Road was on borrowed time.

The shunting in York Road finished, I was welcomed on to No. 62066 to ride the length of this short branch, climbed down at Doncaster Junction, walked a short distance and took the bus back to Doncaster. And do you know? Very few of my colleagues at Gresley House had ever seen the branch and its little yard. Perhaps they went before it closed.

The other branch I explored around this time was quite different. Built at Frodingham by the GC masquerading as the North Lindsey Light Railway (NLLR), it ran due north from a little station at Dawes Lane, located in my time amid the maze of lines where now stood Frodingham loco depot, in the last years of steam. From there the NLLR went through Normanby Park to Winterton & Thealby and on to Winteringham Haven and Whitton, the last two both landings on the bank of the Humber river.

These latter two locations were bleak, windswept places, but both had harboured ambitions of being ports for the iron ore and products of the Frodingham district. The crafty bit was that by building this line, the GCR had secured its place in two totally different sectors, both of which the branch served. One was before my eyes, a heavy traffic on the NLLR to Normanby Park and John Lysaght's steelworks, with block trains of coal and coke, iron ore from Highdyke and Holton le Moor, and steel products coming out. There were two booked pilots at Normanby Park, both 2-8-0s, and they were busy twenty-four hours a day. The next bit was a curiosity, Crosby Mines of the Midlands Ironstone Company, whose own heavy steam shunters pulled home-mined iron ore up and down alongside the NLLR. Crosby Mines signal box itself had an unusual speciality, described for many years in the Appendix to the Working Timetables. This was that 'You might be exposed to blasting there'! When the warning was given (and fairly often it was), the signalman cleared the line and stopped all further traffic, before the agreement procedure was invoked for the mine. When the blasting was finished, the permanent way inspector had to inspect the line for debris and damage before allowing the signal box to reopen. To my regret I was never there when all this happened.

I did, however, spend some time on the Normanby Park pilots, and with the shunters there, a heavy industrial job generating heavy traffics. Lysaghts drove a hard transport bargain, and were not averse to loading steel ingots on to a coaster at Flixbrough Wharf on the Trent, to which they had their own access, to reinforce their negotiating position.

One of the Crosby Mines squat and low profile, but powerful, 0-6-0 saddle tanks. (Bryan Stone)

K1 No. 62063 shunting the 12.15 trip from Frodingham at Winterton, the end of the truncated NLLR. (Bryan Stone)

That brings me to the NLLR's second role. Another would-be competitor had been the Lancashire & Yorkshire (L&Y) Railway, busy shipping coal not far away in Goole. Several times there were threats to bridge (or, once, tunnel under) the lower Trent and penetrate north Lincolnshire. It never happened, but Sir Berkeley Sheffield, a local landowner and member of the GCR Board, decided that it never should. So the GCR made a treaty with the L&Y. As a result the NLLR line went to and from Winteringham and the Haven connection to terminate at Whitton, opened in 1906, with three passenger trains a day, only now remembered in Bradshaw, and almost certainly always a pure loss-maker, and the L&Y stayed at home, as intended. And one happy and sunny day I went past the steel, smoke and ore, and out to the end of the line. No, it was no longer possible in 1964 to get through to Whitton, but I did climb up on 24 January of that year on to No. 62063, another expiring K1, handed down from York and which Frodingham shed thought might, with care, make the 12.55 local goods working out and back.

The trip started at Frodingham No. 2 signal box, where the east curve to Dawes Lane took off. Then we were on the NLLR proper, with eight wagons for Normanby Park. I learned that although block loads ran in and out all day and night, isolated wagons, often of special cargo, still required the pick-up freight. We shunted the train out at Normanby Park, and took on twenty-one wagons to Winterton & Thealby, 6½ miles from Frodingham. These were again shunted out and then, with a few empties, we rolled gently back to Frodingham. Once there I took the early passenger train back to Doncaster. It was not exciting, but it was fascinating, and it gave food for thought that, in this huge industrial complex, we were still tripping odd wagons out to country sidings. Well, it didn't go on much longer. But then, Scunthorpe and Frodingham are no longer what they were.

The next day I was at Dawes Lane when the daily 09.30 Holton le Moor to Normanby Park ironstone pulled into the east curve, and the woefully unprepared 'Austerity' slipped, as it often did, to a stand, helplessly stopping trains, road traffic and work in general. Compared with this, the Winterton pick-up was a leisurely diversion, a lost world. Forty-five years later, in northern Switzerland, I still regret not going out to see what was then still beside the Humber at Winteringham and Whitton.

TRAIN CATERING

Like a number of other career railwaymen, Theo Steel spent time in train catering during a period of great change

I am amazed to realise that over 20 per cent of my career was spent in train catering, from 1975 to 1982. Train catering at the time was part of Travellers' Fare, then an element of British Transport Hotels. Later in the 1980s it was much more directly controlled by the InterCity Sector, complemented by some operations in Network South East and actually increasingly within regional railways, albeit with private contractors taking the risk.

It was a time of great change as HSTs were introduced, first on the Western and then on the Eastern Region. InterCity services were becoming much more frequent – half-hourly to Birmingham, Manchester, Liverpool at the same time, Glasgow electrification and better than hourly to Newcastle and Leeds – all with fixed-formation trains. Electric cooking power succeeded the gas of the Mark I catering vehicles and public tastes were moving fast towards snacks rather than meals.

I spent time on Midland, Western, and Southern routes learning the trade. The Southern buffets were a fascinating operation with drinks left out for regulars to consume on the way home in the evening, with weekly settlement in some instances. The Portsmouth route was notorious for its 'W Club' where drinks were consumed as the train went through each station starting with the letter W! That's five to Guildford. I think, with more to come further on! Sadly, the Brighton Belle had retired by then, but many of the staff were still there.

I was then pitched in to run East Coast from November 1978, just after the route to Edinburgh had been restored following the Penmanshiel tunnel collapse. Times were far from easy and I still have a welcome letter from the then recently appointed general manager, Frank Paterson. My welcome was almost short lived after the same chief steward failed to have a credit card machine with him twice running when Frank was travelling!

Previously the East Coast route was unique for serving more lunches and dinners than breakfasts, although this quickly changed after HSTs were introduced, as customers from as far north as Newcastle came within range for a day return business journey. Amazingly, a new early train from Newcastle was added quickly to the timetable within weeks of the service change.

The first twenty HSTs originally had separate kitchen and buffet vehicles, planned to run with staffs of up to twelve per train. This quickly proved uneconomic and my main job on East Coast Main Line as manager was sorting out staffing and service levels to pull in a deficit which was exceeding staff costs, let alone the cost of materials, as well as restoring quality of service. I recall that we had over 100 per cent staff turnover in 1979 although this settled down as the recession bit. Train catering meals were a renowned barometer of the economy. Director InterCity Cyril Bleasdale was famed for his emphasis on monitoring breakfast numbers served to indicate the business direction!

The pre-HST inheritance on East Coast was a mix of at seat service, first-class Pullmans, and executives (by then there was second-class accommodation on all trains) plus less heavily provided trains with a restaurant seating vehicle. It settled in my time to a few two-catering vehicle formations to cover the key breakfast and dinner trains, complemented by trains with single vehicle facilities. Meal services were generally provided on Anglo Scottish and Newcastle trains and more specifically on the Leeds route.

Again pre-HST, most ECML formations were specific to the train and staff could work on the same catering vehicle for up to a year. This changed totally with HSTs. The need to get unit trains to maintenance meant constant changes of train for staff which had a very challenging effect on management, morale and quality. As each day progressed so the changeovers often mounted.

As you would expect, the best staff settled down quite quickly, but there was a lot of work to do with others working on this very high-profile element of East Coast service with its considerable number of key 'opinion formers' travelling. This was particularly the case from the main non-London markets like Leeds and Newcastle where the core users were a fairly small range of people who knew the key staff well and vice versa. Some of our staff actually worked on State banquets at Buckingham Palace or on civic occasions.

The trains were provided with food and drink at King's Cross, Newcastle and Edinburgh from stores at those stations. There were

Train, station and hotel catering has evolved from the elegant and fanciful era of this illustration to modern fast convenience food provision.

also supply arrangements at Leeds and Hull with the hotels or station catering outlets. Staff were based at these points and at Cleethorpes and York. Before the advent of HSTs many crews lodged, but such arrangements ceased from 1980 as round trips to Edinburgh became the norm. Some trains featured buffet-only services north of Newcastle or Edinburgh. Restaurant cars at weekends ceased from 1980.

The day-to-day challenge was supplemented by some interesting side tasks like operating an all-first-class HST to Norwich in 1978 to celebrate the opening of the Sainsbury Arts Centre at the university there. It was packed with journalists and the family required a 'dry' train. However, thirst was eventually allowed to be quenched, to the great relief of some of the journalists on board!

Filming the catering operation on a speeding train was not without its challenges as I found out when I was involved with the 1978 version of the legendary 'Railway Races to the North'. I travelled with O.S. Nock and James Cameron on almost the last Deltic-hauled Flying Scotsman round trip to Edinburgh. It took over ninety minutes to get the service of 'Brown Windsor' soup correctly filmed and at least three tablecloth changes, as we made good time round the curves along the coast between Edinburgh and Berwick!

There was also at the time a good line in ship launch specials to the Tyne which no one really remembers very clearly! They did provide a superb opportunity for some very talented staff to excel with special menus.

At this period there was very limited on-train communication, which made urgent ordering much more difficult than it is now, even when slow moving through-trains could throw out orders at Peterborough (wedged in a potato so they did not get blown away)!

My time in catering gave me much clearer revenues/costs per train data than was general and served to develop an understanding of balance sheets sooner in my career than most. It also rounded the edges fairly quickly! I am eternally grateful to those who gave me the opportunity to learn and recover from mistakes. It was an amazing period in an intense business, but one still full of incident, like the time the Queen's breakfast had to be rushed along station platforms because of a locked connecting door, or when a King's Cross roof leak flooded our offices and stores.

WE ARE SORRY THAT TRAINS ARE BEING DELAYED DUE TO ADVERSE WEATHER CONDITIONS

During a great storm in 1987 Jim Gibbons encountered a hopeful, but truly unrealistic, passenger

During the night of the 15–16 October 1987 a severe storm across southern England brought thousands of trees down, most of them, it

The great storm in October 1987 put MV *Hengist* aground in the Folkestone Warren. Huge waves at sea nearly capsized her and, losing electrical power, she drifted on to the beach and was badly damaged. (Jim Gibbons)

seemed, across railway tracks. I walked to my local station in complete darkness and climbing over or around a succession of fallen trees in the roads. I used the ETD telephone (fortunately working on its battery) and spoke to the regulator in Three Bridges signalling centre who told me the situation, including the fact that there was no power at all in the box, neither for lighting nor any signalling power supply. All panels were completely dead and Electrical Control HQ at Croydon had confirmed there was no power supply in the whole of south-east England.

I decided to walk to East Croydon, some 2 miles away, and report to the Network Technical Centre. I followed the running line in order to examine those 2 miles as I had no doubt that all lines would need to be examined to determine the degree of blockage and to decide priorities for clearance.

Approximately a mile from my station was South Croydon station and, as I approached it and walked up the ramp on to the platform, I espied a solitary passenger peering down the line and then looking at his watch. I approached him and wished him good morning and asked if he was expecting to catch a train. He replied in the affirmative and commented that 'there seemed to be some delay to the service this morning'.

As tactfully as I could, I pointed out to him that there was not a house, street or any other light in the surrounding area due to a major storm, which seemed to surprise him, and suggested that it would perhaps be best if he returned home. I presumed that like a lot of early morning commuters, he had undertaken the first leg of his journey both on foot and on auto-pilot!

'I HAVE NO COAL'

This was the complaint one of the signalmen made to Terry Worrall when he was area manager at Coventry

Shortly after lunchtime on a cold December day in 1972 I answered my assistant's telephone to find an irate signalman from Gibbet Hill signal box (between Coventry and Kenilworth on the Leamington line) berating me for not having arranged a delivery of coal to the box. He had just come on late turn and threatened to shut the box which, had he done so, would have closed the route between Coventry and Leamington.

After assuring him that I would arrange a delivery, even if I had to deliver it myself, he calmed down and added in a matter-of-fact way, 'And by the way the signal box is on fire.'

I thought I was hearing things and asked him exactly what he meant. He stated that upon taking duty he had noticed that the roof around the stove chimney exit was on fire. He had tried to extinguish it with a water extinguisher. However, as we all know, if a high-pressure water extinguisher is activated towards a hard surface, some 3ft away, its operator will inevitably find himself on the receiving end of a significant proportion of its contents – which this signalman had done and was soaking wet! I instructed him to close the box and leave promptly.

He had not called the fire brigade which I then did via the supervisor in Coventry panel signal box.

The brigade attended quickly and in their attempts to extinguish the fire had to pull most of the roof off the box, as the fire had spread along the tongued-and-grooved interior timber lining of the structure. Fortunately, whilst this incident disrupted the route for days, the box was scheduled to close a fortnight later, when track circuit block signalling was to be implemented along the route.

I always wonder what the signalman might have interpreted as a 'real emergency'!

THE MYSTERY OF HAXBY UP DISTANT

Philip Benham describes a railway whodunnit which nearly upset a very worthwhile idea

The rebuilding work at York station in 1984 included a major facelift to the outer concourse adjacent to the main entrance. The Eastern Region General Manager, Frank Paterson, let it be known that he thought it would benefit from a central feature or artefact. So the search was on to find something suitable.

A few miles outside York on the Scarborough line was Haxby station level crossing, one of two in the village. The crossing was controlled by a gate box with semaphore signals. There was nothing remarkable about this except that the Up line Distant signal was particularly venerable, being of original NER design, with the signal arm fitting inside the 'slotted' wooden post. There were only two of these signals remaining in the York area by this time – the other controlling movements from the Foss Island branch near the Rowntrees factory at Burton Stone Lane signal box.

Someone hit upon the bright idea that Haxby Up Distant would make an ideal centrepiece for the York concourse, and so it was agreed. Come the appointed Sunday in early October, the signalling engineer's staff arrived on site to replace the signal with one of more modern tubular steel design. It was a straightforward enough job which proceeded to plan without a hitch. That is, until it came to transporting the dismantled signal back to the depot at York for refurbishment ready for its new home. Only then was it realised that the post and signal assembly were too big for the road vehicle – a larger lorry would be needed.

The Haxby Up Distant signal in its original location and in the off position for No. 47475 with a Scarborough–Liverpool train. (Philip Benham)

The NER slotted-arm Distant signal from Haxby in its new home on York station concourse. (Philip Benham)

By now the day was drawing on and the decision was made to leave the dismantled signal overnight on the grassy lineside cutting. A big enough vehicle would then recover it the following day. That was just what happened but, unfortunately, over the Sunday night some miscreant had sawn off the signal arm, presumably as a souvenir!

Despite this distasteful setback, shortly afterwards the signal duly appeared in its new place of honour, complete with the coloured arm inside its slotted post very much the focal point. Since then hundreds of thousands of passengers have walked past, little realising that the signal is not quite all it seems.

SOUTHERN WANDERINGS

**Covering stations on a relief basis meant that you
never knew what to expect, as Peter Thomas recalls**

PECKHAM RYE

I went to cover Peckham Rye during the 1954 London bus strike.
All the displaced bus passengers wanted to travel by rail, which
meant that the chief booking clerk, Percy Redford, had to man the
third booking office window while I counted the cash taken. Because
the journeys were mostly local and the fares relatively cheap, most
of it was in coppers. I had to count all this into 5s bags which were
later put into blue linen £20 bags. Then I went up to the platform to
cram hordes of people into already crowded trains, most en route to
Blackfriars or Holborn Viaduct.

At banking time, two of the station staff were recruited to help carry
the large linen bags of cash and we marched down Rye Lane rather
like an African safari. One more job done; time to cross the road to Joe
Lyons for coffee and a buttered bun.

The rest of the day was more normal, apart from the fact that the
shorter working week was now in force and the rest day relief signalman positions were all vacant. With the help of the Redhill relief section we finally got all the boxes covered. Despite all the complications
I enjoyed working at Peckham Rye. At least it was something to get
your teeth into.

UCKFIELD

When I arrived at Uckfield I got a call from the relief section to say that
they were unable to cover Crowborough, so would I take it on. Being
an obliging chap I agreed to do so, although I was already in charge of
Isfield, Barcombe Mills and Culver Junction. I knew that Crowborough
had already dealt with a farm removal during the previous week but,
on arrival there, I found that the leading goods porter was also on leave
and I had to do the stock returns, including a collection of vehicles left
over from the farm removal.

After that, all proceeded normally until the Saturday when the farm removal again entered the scene. I was told that the now empty farm removal vehicles were being returned by the London Midland Region as part of their 'clearing the decks' before a threatened strike by ASLEF members the next day. The special train duly arrived, fully fitted and double-headed. I had borrowed a shunter from Brighton and we decided to split the train, which the shunter would run round ready to place in the Up yard while I dealt with the portion to be placed in the Down yard. Fortunately some help was forthcoming when the fireman of the Brighton did the coupling and uncoupling necessary while I gave hand signals and operated the hand points. When the work was finally completed I got a lift on the engine as far as Uckfield, and enjoyed a mug of the driver's tea on the journey.

BRIGHTON

I went to Brighton in 1956 to familiarise myself with the assistant stationmaster's duties as the then ASM Walter Hill was retiring. The main job was that of the platform working, an art one had to get used to with the large influx of visitors during the summer.

Our measure was to count the thousands of inward ticket halves. When the figure reached 40,000 we knew the evening ahead would be busy. Extra trains were timetabled and there was a standby train, but no guard rostered. We made our plans but, inevitably, the whole operation depended on minute by minute control and action. Tiring, but an excellent prelude to working at Victoria later.

VICTORIA

I went to Victoria in 1959 to be summer assistant stationmaster. There were three regular ASMs and my main task was to produce for printing the copy of the special working book which was published for each Saturday in the summer, based on the special train notices and electric carriage workings. It was a tight timetable to get the book back and out for the station staff to put into operation. Most of the rest of the work was to attend trains, usually on the Central Side.

Working at Victoria was complicated since it was, in effect, two side-by-side stations, a legacy of the 1923 Grouping. The Eastern side platforms Nos 1 to 8 were self-contained and the Central side, platforms 9 to 17 operated a north-to-south system whereby an eight-car train could arrive at the south section while another train in the north section could depart via a middle road.

The principal traffic on the Eastern side was for boat trains, and platforms were reserved at the appropriate time for the Night Ferry, where platform 2 was barricaded off for supervision by HM Customs and Immigration Officers. Platform 8 was similarly reserved for the Golden Arrow. Only platforms 3–6 were electrified, although this eventually was extended to the whole station.

One of the most notable days at Victoria was Derby Day. It started with the Night Ferry which would bring a number of horse-racing fans such as Prince Monolulu the tipster and owner Madame Sozy Volterra, both of whom would attract onlookers hoping to get inside information on the runners.

Fast-forward now to platform 16 which would see the Royal Train. I would go to Stewarts Lane depot and inspect the train and ensure the empty stock train ran in on time. I usually travelled back to Victoria on the train and, on arrival, there was always a group of people in grey top hats en route to the races. Stationmaster Bill Fearne in top hat would be on hand to greet Her Majesty the Queen, who was preceded by other royals intending to travel. All that ended when Derby Day was switched from Wednesday to Saturday and the royal party travelled to the racecourse by road. Happy Days!

Don Love adds:

> When Derby Day was on weekdays I had to have a meeting with the CMEE to beg permission to book all his spare maintenance vehicles into traffic; all traffic stock was in use during peak hours. Permission was always granted, but I ran up a debt of owed favours.
>
> The Tattenham Corner trains were always crowded and there was one that we timed in front of the Royal Train which often ran late, despite our efforts. In such cases it was held at Purley which meant that the punters had to watch the Royal Train go by and then miss the first race. They were not too happy!
>
> I used to tell Commercial Assistant John Colwill that this was an 'operator's day' needing no commercial input and making more

money than a lot of his efforts. I once went to Tattenham Corner myself to 'watch the working' and wore my bowler. The punters on the train thought I was a bookie!

DERAILMENT ON RANNOCH MOOR

Derailments were not new to Jim Dorward's experience, but few involved locations as isolated as Rannoch Moor

It is Wednesday 21 November 1962. Having just arrived for another day in the Glasgow North District Engineer's office in George Square, Glasgow, I am on my way with a permanent way engineer to the derailment of a 10ft wheelbase wagon on the West Highland line, between Tyndrum Upper and Bridge of Orchy. The derailment has happened on the Horse Shoe Curve, where the line turns through 180 degrees in less than a mile. As the location is accessible by road, followed by a walk along a footpath, we are using the office car.

By the time we arrive, the breakdown gang has re-railed the wagon and sent it away. The permanent way inspector (PWI) had decided that the line could reopen, as the track at the point of derailment is just within maintenance tolerance.

So, why did this particular wagon derail? We are currently experiencing a spate of derailments involving four-wheeled wagons with a 10ft wheelbase, such as the standard BR 12-ton covered goods wagon. The problem is exercising the brains of rolling stock and permanent way engineers throughout BR. Why have these wagons, with 'XP' (meaning can be conveyed on express passenger trains) stamped on their sides, started to become derailment prone? I have heard people talking of fast Class C goods trains, such as the Scotch Express, belting along the East Coast Main Line with a 4-6-2 Class A4 steam engine in charge, with no apparent difficulty. Have the suspensions of these wagons become life expired? Are they being unevenly loaded?

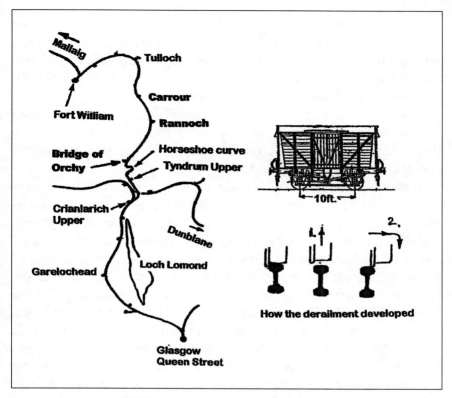

The West Highland line and details of the derailment sequence of 10ft wheelbase wagons. (Jim Dorward)

Are these new diesel locomotives accelerating too fast? Or does the track need to be maintained to a higher standard?

We survey the track in detail, including the measurement of 'voids' under the sleepers. This will enable us to work out its geometry when carrying trains. Although there are voids present under some sleepers, they do not appear to be excessive. So we, the track authority, may be 'off the hook'.

It is now Thursday 22 November and we are in the office trying to confirm that the derailment was not the civil engineer's fault. We then receive word of yet another plain line derailment involving a 10ft wheelbase wagon on the West Highland line. This time it is between Rannoch Moor and Corrour. This is bleak territory, especially in winter, with no road access. We plan a train journey for tomorrow.

The date is now Friday 23 November. Having travelled in to Queen Street station by bus, we are on the 05.55 to Fort William. The sleeping cars from London King's Cross have been attached, along with the all-important restaurant car, where we are to have the full BR breakfast. Something worth getting up for!

About 2 miles north of Rannoch station we look out as the train passes through the snow shed and get ready to detrain. As on Wednesday, the PWI had reopened the single line after the wagon was re-railed and taken away to Fort William.

At about 9.30 a.m. the train stops at Corrour. We are the only souls to get out, which is not surprising, as the only connection with the station is a footpath leading to Loch Ossian. There is snow on the ground and the deer are down at the lineside fence. Dramatic, certainly, but we have to walk back along the line with our equipment to the point of derailment. As on Wednesday, the engineer I am with has now become an expert in such derailments and once again is very doubtful if all the blame can be laid at the civil engineer's door. He is keeping a score card!

We carry out the usual detailed survey and on completion walk back to Corrour station. This must be one of the most isolated stations on BR. The Glasgow train, a welcome sight, arrives about 4 p.m. We climb aboard and make our way along to the restaurant car. We order what we believe to be a very well-earned BR high tea, as we have gathered enough information to prove that this is yet another derailment that is not our fault. The district engineer will be pleased, but where will the next one be and will it be the track's fault? This sort of thing may well be part of a civil engineer's life, but rarely does it involve such isolated locations.

BROAD STREET TERMINUS

Chris Blackman was involved in interesting changes at this once important station

There were four signal boxes for working the Broad Street London terminus, with some very antiquated equipment including Tyers instruments especially adapted for terminal working. There was also a special

146

shunt-out signal at the exit from each platform to release the steam locomotive of each incoming train after its stock had departed on its next working. The tank locomotive thus released would then shunt on to a siding to await the next incoming train to which it would then attach and subsequently take out. The shunt-out signals had served well from the nineteenth century until the end of steam trains.

An intriguing aspect of the interlocking was that it was designed to prevent the next train from entering the platform before the locomotive of the previous one had shunted out of the way. This was a good move by Mr Tyers with safety in mind. However, as the twentieth century progressed and electric multiple unit stock came into use, at least for the Watford and Richmond services, failure to operate the shunt-out signal for a mythical locomotive after the electric train had departed meant that the signalman became locked up and could not set the road for the next train to enter that platform. Being a young and enthusiastic area movements inspector I had naturally taken the trouble to learn the frame and regularly used to work it. At one point in the middle of the rush hour I failed to pull off and put back the beastly shunt-out signal for the ghost locomotive. This caused a few minutes' delay while I reset and re-pulled a dozen or more levers. This delay was duly recorded in the train register, not without some mirth, by Jock Johnstone the signalman.

Incidentally, back in the early 1950s Jock had been a signalman at Harrow No. 2 box, before moving to Broad Street in the 1960s when the power boxes were commissioned and to be nearer his home near Southend. Jock recalled for me the grim day he took late turn duty at Harrow back in 1952 and would never forget the disaster there!

Four months after my arrival Broad Street was rationalised and resignalled. The number of platforms was reduced from nine to five, the number of tracks between Dalston and Broad Street reduced from three or four to two, and Broad Street No. 1, Skinner Street and New Inn Yard boxes were abolished. During the preparatory works in the preceding weeks I had had practical experience in charge of possessions whilst new signals were unloaded and installed. I had also been Responsible Officer/Pilotman for single-line working (SLW) one Sunday between Western Junction (at Dalston) and Broad Street No. 1. This was an interesting task as SLW was also in operation between Western Junction and Dalston Eastern Junction and, accordingly, I wore two pilotman's armbands to be distinguishable from Jack Bates, who was pilotman for the other route.

When the re-signalling weekend came I was booked twelve-hour days on Saturday and Sunday. At the appointed hour of 8 a.m. on Saturday, the Signal & Telegraph technicians started disconnecting all the ancient equipment, and by 2 p.m. the shunt-out signals and all other surplus signals and redundant points had been disconnected or secured. When the afternoon shift arrived I paused for a bite to eat and cup of tea. At this point there was the sound of footsteps coming up the steps of Broad Street No. 2, so I moved to the entrance door to challenge the new arrivals.

'We've come for the instruments,' the person said.

'That's as may be, but who are you?' I asked.

'I'm from the museum.'

'Oh, yes, which one?'

At which point one of the new arrivals fumbled around in his overalls and produced a requisition document from Clapham Museum. A couple of phone calls confirmed authenticity, and, refreshed by a cup of tea, they proceeded to cart away Mr Tyers's ancient handiwork. To the best of my knowledge the instruments are now in the care of York National Railway Museum.

The rest of the weekend went smoothly and by close of play on Sunday the new signalling and layout, including a new set of motor points, had been tested and formally commissioned.

I was back at 6 a.m. on the Monday together with Jock Johnstone. As Jock had a doctor's appointment on the following day, he had been booked a day's leave and so a special class relief signalman had also taken duty to learn the new signalling ready for Tuesday. There were a couple of small problems as the new signalling bedded in, but for a while all went well until, in contravention of instructions issued, the first train from the Eastern Region arrived with a Brush Type 2 diesel on the front. Immediately the block went on any further trains from the Eastern as there was no way of running round, nor any other locomotive to take the empty stock away. That there was no longer a shunt-out signal was the least of our concerns!

Shortly after this there was a problem with clearing the signal for a train out of the new platform 1 via the motorised crossover. I went down to the platform ready to hand-signal the train if required.

'OK to proceed. Tell the driver to pass the signal at danger,' shouted the relief signalman.

'Is the road correctly set?' I asked.

'Yes,' replied the relief man.

I instructed the driver accordingly to proceed cautiously and to pass the signal at danger. I unfurled and exhibited a green flag and off he went. A few seconds later there was an urgent yell from Jock from the signal box window, 'Stop him, he's going wrong road, the crossover is not reversed.' Armed only with a green flag, I remembered the rule drummed into me (and which until then I had thought spurious) that a green flag waved violently indicates danger. Never have I waved a green more violently and agonisingly!

Fortunately the guard, who had been looking out, witnessed my exhibitionism and applied the brake and simultaneously the driver, proceeding cautiously, had reached the motor crossover, realised that something was wrong, and slammed on the anchors. We set the train back and at the second attempt got it safely away. I decided to deal with the incident straight away, gave the relief signalman a few choice words which he accepted with good grace and some relief, and that was the end of the matter.

TAKING THE MARKS

'Taking the marks' to classify a signal box Chris Blackman found varied from incredibly boring to highly entertaining

When I arrived at Willesden as area movements inspector (AMI) in 1969 I ascertained the grading classification of each of the thirty-four signal boxes, and was amazed at the mismatch between the allocated grade and the current workload and responsibility. I sat in Western Junction box at Dalston watching the peak hour traffic with seven trains an hour each way on the No. 2 lines (Dc electrified), a similar number on the No. 1 lines carrying DMUs (Diesel Multiple Units) from Finsbury Park heading to Broad Street, and the occasional freight to or from the Victoria Park direction. Each of the four lines to Canonbury station had an Intermediate Block signal – yes, there were IB signals 'in rear' controlled by Western Junction! – and I considered that the signalmen Charlie Jennings, Arthur Page and Laudie Dieah deserved their grading of Special B, even if Laudie hit the block bells with the ferocity of a sledgehammer. On the other hand, halfway between Dalston and Broad Street was Dalston Dunloe Street which had no crossover and just a Home and Distant signal in each direction on two lines, but the signalmen there were still graded Special Class. Admittedly during the peak couple of hours there was a steady stream of trains, but each one only required at most four lever movements and in many cases only two, as frequently there was insufficient opportunity to pull the Distant off. The grading at Dunloe Street was a relic of the days when there had been four tracks with Home, Starter and Distant in each direction and a lot more point-work and signals. The signal box had not been re-marked, protected by a 'Standstill' agreement negotiated back in the war, whereby box grading could not be reviewed until March 1971.

A particular concern of mine was Gospel Oak No. 3, which was graded as Class 3, and deemed therefore to be suitable for a candidate straight out of signalling school. As well as the regular twenty-minute electric Broad Street–Richmond service, there were a number of freights, some of which came off the Tottenham & Hampstead line, known simply as the T&H. In effect Gospel Oak was a converging point for North London line freights heading west to the Euston, Paddington and Southern Region lines. Gospel Oak to Kensal Green was a vital artery on the route, so this necessitated careful regulation and dialogue with Kensal Green Junction. There were regularly one or two freights in the gap between each electric service and on one occasion, with an experienced Special Class relief signalman at each end, I saw four freights packed in with no damage to the twenty-minute frequency of the passenger service!

The signalman's Local Departmental Committee requested that the marks at Gospel Oak be taken and accordingly one of the inspectors from Divisional Office attended from 6 a.m. to 6 p.m. and I did the twelve-hour night shift. The task included counting the number of lever movements made. My company that night was signalman Danny Keane, an entertaining Class 1 relief man who hailed from the Emerald Isle. Although in the early hours there was nothing more than a steady stream of freights off the branch from the T&H, Danny insisted on resetting and normalising the junction points to the main line (i.e. towards Camden Road) after each train in order to keep up the count of lever movements. I marked accordingly as I confess that I would have been content to see the box regraded to Class 2. However, our efforts were to no avail; it just missed reaching the necessary mark for regrading.

Taking the marks at Watford Power Box was different. The magic scoring figure was simply a function of the box's equipment mark and the number of trains that passed each shift. The box equipment was assessed by Divisional Chief Inspector Peacock from the signal box plans and sitting in the warmth of the office at Eversholt Street near Euston. The count of trains was done by the inspectors. The local AMI at Watford naturally elected to do the twelve-hour day shift, and so 'Muggins' at Willesden drew the short straw again and was delegated to do twelve-hour nights. Once the Dc lines finished at midnight and stock had been shunted off to Croxley, it was just the main lines with sleeping car trains, Freightliners and some ordinary freights, although engineering work around Berkhamsted necessitated some switching Fast to Slow etc. I continued to tick off the trains as they passed, and as the signalman became more absorbed in his newspaper I started to work the box. The signalman from time to time ticked off trains while I kept an eye on what he was doing. At the end of the shift I added up the trains, despatched the sheets to Divisional Office and caught the train home.

A few days later I was summoned to Euston to see Divisional Operating Officer Jock Callaghan, who had a reputation as a fiery ex-chief inspector and, before that, an officer in the Black Watch regiment. Apparently there had been a dispute with the NUR over the result of the marks taking. This had led to a close inspection of the records, which revealed a clear distinction between the ticks in the early part of the shift and those ticks in the night hours. The ensuing Black Watch interrogation would have broken the most hardened German spy, and before long I duly admitted that for part of the time I had been working the box while the signalman had been ticking off the trains as they passed. 'But I was closely watching him,' I murmured. This cut no ice with JC, who explained to me in robust manner the errors of my ways, that I had been sent to do a particular job and no other, especially not having a go at working the panel. No ifs, no buts, just 'the way out is behind you'. I did a hasty about-turn and, duly chastened, made for the door. As I turned the door knob, JC looked up from his desk and said softly, 'Oh, by the way, Chris, did you enjoy yourself working the panel?'

I grinned and left!

THE BLACK MAC

Chris Blackman's uniform mac, that prerequisite for an inspector, was nearly his undoing

A few months after I arrived at Willesden I had acquired plenty of experience on the track in all weathers and was familiar with the hazards of third-rail, and indeed fourth-rail, electrified lines. Stepping across tracks fitted with a live rail was a necessary everyday occurrence, and I soon stopped being scared of the 'juice' rail. However, one day when wearing a long black mac in a torrential rainstorm, I crossed the tracks near New Inn Yard just outside Broad Street, and overlooked the fact that, when stepping right across the juice rail and the neighbouring running rail, the bottom of the mac was closer to the ground than normal; any kid with a knowledge of geometry could tell you that! And so it happened that 650 volts ran up the back of the mac and hit me just behind the ears. It was a stunning reminder that I was once bottom of the form in geometry, and furthermore a salutary lesson that I should never relax personal vigilance when on the track!

DI DAD

Gerry Orbell was very proud of and greatly influenced by his district inspector father

Gerry Orbell's father joined the London & North Eastern Railway as a lad porter at the age of 16 in 1929 at Coldham station, and spent as much time as possible in the signal box there. In 1937 he obtained a job as porter-signalman at Acle which was combined with that of resident crossing keeper. His wife (my mother) operated the cross-

Wearing his DI's bowler hat, Henry Orbell talks to BRB Chairman Sir Richard Marsh at March. (*Cambridgeshire Times*/Gerry Orbell)

ing when Henry was on duty as porter-signalman. The bells, gongs and indicators between the signal boxes were repeated in mother's kitchen and when she had an indication that a train was coming, she went out and closed the gates across the road. She then went to the frame of levers between the track and the house, locked the gates, and lowered the interlocked signals for the appropriate direction.

Henry progressed through a variety of posts and, in 1958, was selected out of 110 applicants for the post of district inspector, located at Peterborough East. His area covered parts of former LMS, M&GN, GE and GN lines – all of which, despite nationalisation, still had a number of differing operating rules. Gerry recalls how proud his father was to wear his well-earned bowler hat.

Henry's new post involved him in major highway projects on the route of the old A1 road, including crossing the Kettering line, a new stretch at Wansford and the Stamford bypass. The Wansford job, for example, involved a new bridge requiring eighty, 40ft concrete beams brought in by two steam locomotives from Spital shed hauling a weight of around 800 tons. In the Stamford job, thousands of tons of soil and major piling work for a 20ft-high embankment – all involving contractors' movements over a temporary level crossing – had to be supervised. All big jobs for a newly appointed DI.

Another task for Henry occurred when a bad accident happened to a freight train in stormy weather on the ER-LM border between Seaton Junction and Barrowden & Wakeley. There, the embankment slipped after the engine and ten or so wagons had passed over, but the middle section of the train – comprising loaded coal wagons, vanfits and a tank-wagon – slipped down the bank. The rear of the train and the brake van remained on the track, and although the guard was shaken he, with the stoicism inherent in railway staff, protected the accident with detonators.

Once the Up line was opened, the steam cranes were able to work, with very many trains unloading their wagons of ballast and other material to rebuild the bank. After this the steam cranes dragged all the loaded wagons from the water up the newly formed bank. The line reopened after a couple of days, with a temporary speed restriction in operation.

Gerry also remembers how meticulous his father was in establishing the cause of every accident he attended. Henry was noted, too, for his strong empathy with staff and his well-attended evening classes in rules and regulations which often brought out friendly rivalry between signalmen and footplate staff, and between the staff and himself. He was also involved extensively with the MOT (Ministry of Transport) Inspectorate in establishing the first level crossing autobarriers in East Anglia, in supervising the engine changing at March for summer weekend excursions, in work on increasing line capacity between Ely and Brandon, dealing with the destruction by fire of the Nene bridge near Peterborough and in special work on the Whitemoor Yard hump wagon retarders. Henry was a fair man of wide experience, devoted to his job and to helping others do theirs.

The Up Yard control tower at Whitemoor marshalling yard with Arthur Randall at the points switchboard and Wally Storey operating the retarders. (*Cambridgeshire Times/* Gerry Orbell)

The Black Bridge over the River Nene at Peterborough was destroyed by fire in June 1963. On the left of this picture a new line on a trestle bridge is nearly ready for opening. (*Cambridgeshire Times/*Gerry Orbell)

THE EUSTON
BACKING-OUT ROADS

Chris Blackman could only watch in horror as a coupling began to lift off its hook at the top of the Camden bank

At the foot of Camden bank on the Down side lay the so-called 'backing-out' roads. In 1970 they were mostly used for the purpose of backing in a train from the Down side shed into the station. The procedure for this propelling move was that the guard or shunter would bring the empty stock train to a stand at the signal at the bottom of the bank by applying the brake in the leading coach. When the signal was cleared for the stock to proceed into the station, the shunter would release the brake and the driver, upon seeing the brake released, would apply power and propel into the station. The irregular part of the operation was when the shunter used a matchbox or something similar to keep the brake applied. If the matchbox were crushed and the brake leaked off, the driver would start to propel; then, if the signal was still at danger, the train would go through the trap points and be derailed.

I was called out one cold night early in 1970 to attend one such derailment of two coaches. The locomotive had drawn off the remainder of the train and stowed the vehicles back in the Down side shed. Meanwhile the Willesden breakdown train had arrived and taken up position on the Down Slow line. The crane was not required as it was an opportunity to use the new German jacking equipment, which avoided the need for electrical isolation. After liaising with the supervisor, I arranged for the 350hp shunt loco from the shed to approach and stand clear, ready to remove the vehicles as they were re-railed. Then it was a matter of waiting and watching as the breakdown crew got on with it.

Half an hour later the first vehicle was re-railed, checked by the fitters and declared fit to be moved away pending detailed inspection at the depot. I instructed the shunter and driver to couple up and then draw it up the bank to the Down side shed. Meanwhile, I walked up the bank to check with the Down side shed inspector where he wanted the vehicle to be stabled. Having established that, I turned and watched the shunt engine crawl slowly up the bank towards me with the first re-railed coach trailing behind. I signalled to the driver to stop so that I could give him and the shunter the next instruction. As the movement came to a stand, the coach buffered up gently to the locomotive and I could see the screw coupling between locomotive and coach start to lift off the hook of the coach. At the same instant I noticed, to my horror, that the shunter had not connected the brake pipe. Moreover, this vehicle was not fitted with a handbrake, and was thus at risk of running away back down the bank to collide with the next coach being re-railed. Worse still, it would endanger the lives of the breakdown crew busy re-railing the remaining coach.

I held my breath. After what seemed an eternity, but in retrospect was barely a second, the coupling resettled itself on the hook of the coach. I breathed again and came out in a cold sweat at the prospect of what might have been. The remaining vehicle, when re-railed, came up the bank with the shunter riding in it and the brake pipe properly connected! The shunter had learnt a lesson, but the shunt engine driver should have known better. I reflected on the fact that you cannot rely on staff always to carry out duties correctly, and that I perhaps should have made sure that the coupling procedures had been fully carried out.

AN ARRESTING SCENE

Jim Summers experienced the fallout when a nervous producer got himself overexcited during a film shoot

A stranger bustled into the pokey wee office of the duty container terminal regulator, the fancy name for the shift foreman of the new integrated road/rail/sea service. Brand new, it had become the eighth wonder of the world. 'I'm the cameraman,' he said with a nod and a wink, whispering confidentially, 'but another chap will come in shortly and tell you he's the producer. Pay no heed to him.' He then vanished, and the next intrusion was indeed the producer, who outlined his wishes; clearly an artistic type.

It was to be an important film, putting British Railways in a good light and showing what it was doing for the export drive; so important in fact that one of the shift regulators was taken off normal duties to see to it that every whim of the film crew was catered for. Simple.

So how could I manage to end up on the carpet in the Shipping & Port Manager's office?

It had all hinged on timing. The storyline depended upon the container ship arriving at Parkeston from Zeebrugge on schedule, the hatches would then be opened, the large transporter crane would dive in and the first container to come out would be *the* one with a mysterious cargo. Actually, to be sure, we had pre-loaded it at Parkeston on the outward voyage, so it had made a round trip. You get one chance at this sort of scene, so we left nothing to chance, as it were. We even ensured the vessel's chief engineer failed that particular hatch cover at Zeebrugge to prevent our colleagues there from taking the special container out unintentionally. And so we were full of confidence when the ship entered the river early in the morning to sail up to her berth and be recorded on film. The sun had risen and was in the right position for shooting. The water was like a millpond. The perfect scene. The producer was ecstatic. 'Get on that crane and get a shot of the ship coming alongside,' he instructed the cameraman.

Now 'that crane' was one of our two transporters, a Stothert & Pitt affair, capable of lifting 30-ton containers from its height of 140ft. If you were up there, you could feel it dip as it took the strain. It could travel sideways along the quay to align with the cells in the ships' holds, as well as traverse in and out with the containers. A vertical ladder went up one of the legs to enable the crane driver to get up to his eyrie.

The cameraman got on the ladder, climbed a couple of steps and prepared to film the ship, now getting pretty close.

'Higher,' commanded the producer. The cameraman climbed a further couple of steps and again prepared to shoot.

'No, higher!' shouted the producer.

Slowly the cameraman went a bit higher, but not high enough for the stunning aerial shot envisaged by the producer. 'Higher! Higher!' he bawled, seeing the ship getting ever closer. As I said, you get one chance at this sort of shot.

The cameraman played his ace card. 'Can't hear you,' he shouted down. 'You'll need to come up and show me!' The producer gulped

– the things you do for art – and stepped on to the lowest rung. Nervously and shakily, he managed three or four more, at which point the crane started to move sideways. He went white with fear; he had no head for heights, let alone for hanging on to a moving crane. The crane was positioning itself for the berthing ship, which was now not far from coming alongside. Bathed in beautiful early morning sunshine, the quay was clear. It should have been the perfect shot, if only the cameraman had been right up that crane.

Unfortunately, a British Transport policeman chose that moment to plod across the quay. It was unwise for the white-knuckled producer, now near-hysterical, to explode and bawl, 'P**s off, you old fool!' Very unwise, for the policeman booked him! Meanwhile the cameraman nipped up to the top of the crane and captured the ship coming gracefully alongside.

The film company wrote to the Shipping & Port Manager enquiring as to how it could happen that one of its producers could come under the notice of the police while going about his business of making a film under the care of an experienced regulator. As the S&PM said to me, rather pointedly, 'A good question!'

BARGING IN

Geoff Body's return to the place where his original railway appointment interview took place resulted in some surprises as well as nostalgia

The former district goods and passenger manager's office at Peterborough was housed in a severe and forbidding GNR building which matched the old station and the Great Northern Hotel for unrelieved ugliness. Even so, when I returned to the area many years later I was pleased to see the old place still there and used by a few of those familiar railway outcasts who could not be found proper accommodation elsewhere. I now had a freight sales responsibility for the area and no one questioned my right to poke about in the offices I had once found so intimidating.

My first find was a copy of the former district manager's comments on my first report as a traffic apprentice. I had been sent to Spalding,

There were many close links between railways and canals. Here the Down Welshman with twelve somewhat mixed coaches passes a loaded narrowboat heading sedately south near Brinklow.

which was one of his stations, and his report on my progress was quite complimentary. I smiled when I read the claim that those suggestions I had made for improvements 'were already in hand'. The implication was that they had already been thought of. Even district managers needed to present well, it seemed.

The second find was a batch of papers that cast a fascinating light on railway activity in the eastern counties a century earlier. The report and letters it contained went right back to early LNER and pre-grouping days. That was a time when not only were railways at their zenith, but the network of waterways that linked the River Nene with most of the fenlands to the east of Peterborough was busy with barges and lighters. In addition to a certain amount of local traffic, the barging firms were frequently employed in bringing loads for longer distance journeys into a suitable railway station where facilities existed for the transfer of the traffic into wagons for onward rail carriage. An excellent piece of co-operation between differing transport agencies, it seemed. Unfortunately, as I read more of my new-found 'archive', it seemed that there was clearly a fly in the proverbial ointment.

Peterborough was very much a transport gateway to East Anglia. It was served by four pre-grouping railways and bridged the River Nene, itself an important artery between the Fens and Northampton. There was a Great Eastern riverside wharf at Stanground, where the Nene and its inlets was almost alongside the GER Peterborough East station. The former Midland company also had a local wharf to link with its route to Stamford and points beyond, and the London & North Western line due west to Rugby and Northampton had riverside facilities at Woodstone, or Woodston, Wharf. What a tempting set-up for bringing traffic out from the heart of the eastern counties empire of Great Eastern area lines to one of the LMS-group wharves at Peterborough, even though there were perfectly suitable depots much nearer where it could be loaded direct to rail. No wonder rates manipulation and consequent angry exchanges between railway officers became rife, with the Midland, in particular, active and even offering free barging for goods brought into their Peterborough empire. And my file showed the LNER company to be extremely unhappy about this, but it all made fascinating reading.

The problems apparently began back in 1883 when the GN, GE, Midland and L&NW companies started offering free boatage on waterways to persuade them to use their own route traffic offering pretty well anywhere that had water access, which is quite a lot of places in Fenland. Only coal, coke and bricks were excluded. After suffering this crippling competition for a time, common sense prevailed and they collectively agreed upon a 'pooling' arrangement. This provided for the receipts from agreed places and traffics to be recorded and then divided, after allowances for out-payments and working expenses, in proportion to a sensible assessment of actual movements which was undertaken in the years 1899, 1900 and 1901.

Like most such agreements this worked well at first and, along with others of its kind, was 'frozen' during the First World War. However, it came up for scrutiny again in 1928, seemingly because the Midland, now vested in the LMS, was still doing special deals. Examples included grain, hay and straw barged up the River Witham to the LMS waterside facility in Lincoln and loads from deep in ex-Great Eastern territory at Littleport barged free to the LMS wharf at Stanground. My file also noted, in passing, that the LMS had a crane there but would not let anyone else use it!

From the figures quoted it was clear that the Fen Pool, as this arrangement was called, worked against the LNER. However, it was decided not to take any action, apparently because the company did much better from various other pools in existence and feared to disturb the overall position. It was all fascinating reading and made me aware that at least a dozen of these pools had existed and, for all I knew, lasted right up to nationalisation. What stories and intrigue lay behind such pools as the Birmingham Iron & Steel Pool, the Liverpool Timber, Carlisle & London Meat and Norfolk & Suffolk Livestock ones, I wonder?

GUARDING THE FIFE COAST EXPRESS

Spotting an emerging problem, Hugh Gould had to do some quick re-plotting of guards' workings to solve it

For some years after the Second World War, the Fife Coast Express (St Andrews–Glasgow Queen Street) was operated with the pre-war Silver Jubilee set which had been stored at Ballater during the war but was without the restaurant triplet of vehicles. The train was brought to Glasgow in the morning by a Thornton depot guard, but going back at 4.05 p.m. it was rostered for an Edinburgh guard (they went everywhere!) who had travelled to Glasgow as a passenger, 'On the Cushions', except on Mondays and Fridays when he worked a relief train to the North Briton to Leeds.

One Monday afternoon, I was in Cowlairs Yard on the empty coaching stock for the 16.37 to Alloa when I noticed the relief North Briton going the wrong way – down through Springburn towards Queen Street Low Level – probably due to congestion upstairs! But unless they had remembered to provide a relief guard to take the Leeds empty train away from the Low Level, where it could not be terminated, the Edinburgh guard would be off on a grand tour of the western suburbs of Glasgow and was highly unlikely to be back at Queen Street in time for his 'Fifer'.

I crossed my fingers and plotted. By 4 p.m. I was sitting in Queen Street in my Alloa train. On the next platform was the Silver Jubilee set with five minutes to go and no guard. I mentioned this to the foreman who, true to form, had not noticed. Panic.

I said, 'This is what we will do. I will take the "Fifer" to St Andrews, and empty train to Leuchars, then work the 17.15 ex-Aberdeen from Leuchars and on to Edinburgh. When George Campbell comes on duty he can take my Alloa train and finish my turn (which is boring except for the Alloa trip anyway). When the Edinburgh guard reappears, he can take George's 17.00 to Edinburgh, empty train to Craigentinny, and finish. When I get to Waverley with the Aberdeen train, I will come home with George's 22.20 service.'

And that is exactly what we did. George got home early, the Edinburgh guard got home early and I got a little overtime, plus an imaginary medal from the foreman. And, because I always carried my box camera, I also got a photograph of the Silver Jubilee coaches taken from the guard's van.

So, we all lived happily ever after. Not quite. The 17.17 from Aberdeen was loaded heavily with mail, which the Edinburgh men knew how to sort. I did not, so when we reached Waverley it was all in one heap in the middle of the van. I retreated to the sound of disgruntled, chorusing postmen! Well, you can't win 'em all!

CLOSURE CHALLENGE

Bill Parker and a group of colleagues from other departments were tasked to examine some Beeching closure plans

As divisional operating superintendent, Euston Division and assistant divisional manager, Birmingham, I found myself in the lead in dealing with some of the closure proposals in the Beeching Report and others appropriate for evaluation. It was clear from the supporting information that some of the lines listed for closure were not worth fighting for, such as the Verney Junction–Buckingham branch. These hardly warranted the heavy burden of producing information for the laid down closure consultation procedure. In other cases, however, even from a quick examination, the evidence was clearly flawed. The finance officers in my group were, fortunately, knowledgeable mathematicians, a subject in which I have always felt competent too.

The branch lines we decided to concentrate our closure challenge on were Watford Junction to St Albans Abbey, Watford High Street to Croxley, Bletchley to Bedford St Johns and Birmingham to Stratford-upon-Avon. Data for each was collected, the figures carefully scrutinised, traffic and cost forecasts made and judgements, bred of experience, applied. We became increasingly aware of the real situation and prospects, and of how costs and revenue might be improved in each case.

The Beeching proposals did not only highlight the clear need for some closures, but also generated thought and action on worthwhile changes that would produce improvements in other situations. One example was the provision of a new, simple station at Garston in the developing area of Watford, something the local authority was enthusiastic about and prepared to support financially. Another was singling and signalling cost reduction between Bletchley and Bedford plus a link for through running between Bedford St Johns and Bedford Midland, although these did have to wait for a time due to network-wide investment restraints.

With the support of our divisional managers, Leslie Leppington, Jumbo Williams and John Pollard, our figures were presented to regional and BR headquarters and were accepted, with just the hint of a suggestion we had 'fiddled the books'. Did we do the right thing in this rescue operation? Results can answer that question. The current user of the St Albans branch has now shot up to something like a million passengers a year, there are thoughts of extending the Croxley branch westwards to Rickmansworth and the Bedford Midland connection has been made, along with some singling of the line. Stratford-on-Avon station has a vast car park and it is nearly always full to capacity and the old route from there to Honeybourne has become a candidate for reinstatement. These are all success stories, so thank goodness we made our challenges.

MRS CARTER'S
LAST GOODBYE

An initial contact with Mike Lamport and a lot of goodwill from railwaymen allowed an old lady a touching farewell

In the autumn of 1994, as British Rail was fragmenting and I was public affairs manager for Network SouthEast's West Anglia & Great Northern Train Operating Unit, I received a call from local radio personality and former BR man, Richard Spendlove. Richard, who at that time presented a hugely popular phone-in and music programme on BBC Radio Cambridgeshire, had received a request for help from a listener who lived 'just over the border' in the Suffolk village of Thurston, just east of Bury St Edmunds. It was on behalf of 99-year-old Mrs May Carter whose son Brian had been born with an incurable heart defect (known as a 'Blue Baby') and sadly died in September 1950 at the age of 23, a few years after the family had moved from Carmarthen to Lincolnshire. Her son's one pleasure was watching the trains go by. Initially this was from his father's creamery overlooking the GWR station at Carmarthen, and later, alongside the four-tracked East Coast Main Line near Essendine, just north of Peterborough.

On learning of Brian's death, his father's former employees at the United Dairies Carmarthen Creamery clubbed together to fund a memorial stone which BR agreed would stand, facing the tracks on the Up side of the ECML, inside the railway fence close to Milepost 87. However, its location meant that any return visit seemed out of the question as it would have involved trespassing on to the railway. So, how was Mrs Carter going to able to pay her respects to her son for one last time?

Richard, who had been stationmaster at Essendine before it closed in 1959, put me in touch with a number of railwaymen on his old patch including Arthur Cook, who was then a crossing keeper for Railtrack at nearby Tallington box. At the same time I sounded out Railtrack, British Rail Infrastructure Services, East Coast Trains and Anglia Railways, all of whom readily agreed to co-operate to make a unique and very personal visit possible.

Mrs Carter, with the white stick, sees her son's lineside memorial for the first time in forty-five years. With her are friends and, left to right with the umbrellas, Richard Spendlow, Mike Lamport and Arthur Cook. (Mike Lamport)

So, on a very wet Tuesday, 13 December 1994, Richard and I travelled by train to Thurston where we, Mrs Carter and her friend Mrs Ivy Twydale joined Anglia Railways' 09.43 Ipswich–Peterborough service, which made a special stop for us. On arrival at Peterborough a car was waiting to take us to the memorial site deep in the countryside, alongside the East Coast Main Line.

On arrival we were met by Kevin Groves, of Railtrack ECML, who introduced us to BRIS colleagues Dougie Daff and Reg Windsor from the local track maintenance gang. Dougie and Reg had spent a great deal of time and effort in removing a section of lineside fencing and laying a sleeper access walkway across rough ground. They had even planted some fresh flowers around the memorial to add a little colour to this otherwise bleak December day. All of these efforts did not go unnoticed by Mrs Carter as she stood silently and tearfully in front of her son's memorial, which she had not seen for over forty years and would never see again.

All in all this was a magnificent effort by railway people who, although in the midst of re-organisational turmoil, could still find the time to help a mother to realise a last wish which, only by everyone working together, could come to pass.

THE LAST JOURNEY

Geoff Body closes this third collection of railway stories with a fictional piece which nevertheless captures a period when the railway wagon fleet was still a motley collection of all types, ages, origins and ownership

'Oh no; not a grease box,' is the way I've been greeted for some years now. Just because I'm a rather ancient railway wagon and my axle boxes use thick grease for lubrication. It's rather like being an Edwardian. People are just not quite sure what that entails, but are suspicious. Right; the facts are that I am a normal 13-ton capacity, 4-wheeled open wagon with medium sides, totally typical of thousands that were the mainstay of the railway movement of general goods for over half a century. But now, in my dotage, modern railwaymen want to load traffic into wagons with oil axle boxes, or even the new-fangled ones with roller bearings. So much for my useful life of service!

Roller bearings! Whatever will they think of next? And why this prejudice against tried and tested equipment? I do believe it's because some regulator-happy locomotive drivers run too fast so that my axles overheat and the surrounding grease smoulders and eventually bursts into flame. The 'Stop and Examine Train' bell signal is then sent and the observant signalman notes 'Hot Box' in his train register. Back go the boards, the train comes to a standstill and I am shunted ignominiously into some remote siding to cool down. There I shall undoubtedly wait for ages for some disgruntled Carriage & Wagon man to emerge from his canteen comforts for the messy task of cleaning me up. Of course, the train I was on is now running late and the tearaway driver will have to wait for his 'snap' break. Serve him right!

Change had to come though. The heady years of being needed are past and I am now a hunted creature. The word is out that I and the few of my kind still at work are 'to be taken out of service', which is a euphemistic way of describing being hauled off to some out-of-the-way scrapyard. There my timbers will be burned off and my wheels and underframe consigned to some furnace in the smoky parts to the north. Ugh!

Actually, I had successfully kept away from wagon inspectors and number-takers for some time by hiding on the remote Norfolk agricultural network known as the Wissington Light Railway, which wanders about the Fens far from official scrutiny. I had arrived at Downham Market with a load of machinery spares for the sugar beet factory beside the River Wissey. The following day the morning goods from King's Lynn picked me up and, after calling at the junction at Denver, turned east along the single line branch towards Stoke Ferry. At the former Abbey station I was left in the sidings to await collection by one of the British Sugar Corporation's locomotives. Eventually an ancient 0-6-0 saddle tank fetched me to the factory unloading point and I was relieved of my machinery items.

Beyond the factory a crazy network of roadside rail tracks wandered on, with half a dozen branches probing about the flat lands in the huge open space between the Great and Little Ouse rivers. This, I was to learn, was the Wissington Light Railway, which had been hugely

Thirty-two years after its regular passenger train service ended, Stoke Ferry station still has a complement of three luggage barrows. An empty wagon – with grease axle boxes? – stands near the buffer stops, but the station cat is the only sign of life.

important to the Ministry of Food in the war years, conveying sugar beet to the factory and other produce yielded by that dark, fertile soil. Presumably a wagon had been ordered by one of the Fenland farmers for outwards loading and my next move was to be rattled on towards one of the simple wooden loading bank platforms which had been erected at various spots along this tortuous light railway network. When the track had last been levelled or the grass along its roadside routes trimmed was anybody's guess and it is a wonder that neither I nor my wheezing tank locomotive was derailed on our journey. But, we arrived safely. I was eventually set back into a short siding and there I stayed for the next few months, the original purpose behind my arrival apparently forgotten. It was all very pleasant really. Lonely, yes, but warm and peaceful. Turnips mind their own business and have no interest in making old wagons redundant.

Thus things stayed until the fateful day of what was to be my last journey arrived and the daydreams of my respectable and useful past were rudely interrupted. My new load was empty drums which had once held tractor fuel and I was hauled back to the junction with the

Stoke Ferry branch by one of the local saddle tanks and then moved on to Downham Market to wait for the Lynn pick-up. This was a local train which pottered from station to station dropping inwards traffic, doing the shunting and picking up the outwards loads. Actually, it was quite pleasant to be back at work and the journey to Ely was quite an uncomplicated adventure. Even the move on to Whitemoor marshalling yard was not too bad, but there things all went pear-shaped!

When it opened between the wars Whitemoor was an LNER showpiece, the latest in marshalling yard practice, and exchanging and re-sorting traffic between the former Great Eastern system and the rest of the country. It was still doing this job efficiently at the time I arrived and my train was duly placed in the Down reception sidings to await attention. Off went the locomotive to March Shed and we wagons were noted down and our type and destination recorded on a 'cut card' which would then be passed on to the control tower. This was located at the top of the 'Hump', an artificial rise over which the arrivals, duly uncoupled at the right places and in the right groups, were propelled at a steady speed by a Class 08 diesel shunter. Using the information on the cut cards, the wagons for the various destinations then ran down the slope towards the departure sidings with sufficient space in between them to be directed by the control operators into the 'road' appropriate to their destination. Power-operated points and hydraulic 'retarders' were used to route each cut and then to slow it down sufficiently to avoid violent impact on preceding wagons.

All very impressive but, unfortunately, I had been feeling increasingly warm down below for some time and the rapid descent down the hump proved the last straw. I was a 'Hot Box' again! Instead of being drawn down to the departure area for a quiet rest before resuming my journey and safely away from the prying eyes of the number-takers, I was spotted by one of the 'wagon chasers', hooked on to the yard pilot and hustled away to the C&W sidings. A 'Not To Go' notice was slapped on my mainframe and I knew it was all over. I would be compared with the 'wanted' list and any chance of a comfortable retirement at some preservation centre was now a forlorn hope.

If you enjoyed this book, you may also be interested in …

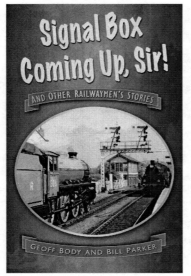

Signal Box Coming Up, Sir!
GEOFF BODY AND BILL PARKER

There's never a dull moment as Geoff Body and Bill Parker present often-hilarious highlights from the careers of railwaymen around Britain over the last fifty years. Featuring daring robberies, royal visits, lost passengers, bomb scares, coffins, circus trains and ladies of the night, it chronicles both successes and disasters, with accounts of moving a farm and a circus, 245 miles of marooned railway, footplate adventures, animal capers and many equally fascinating subjects.

9780752460406

Firing the Flying Scotsman and the Other Great Locomotives
KEN ISSITT

Fast train fireman Ken Issitt worked on the footplate from the late 1940s to 1960, experiencing firing some of the greatest locomotives from the *Flying Scotsman* to *Coltimore* and *Blink Bonney*. The work was hard and conditions were tough but little did Ken know at the time that he was experiencing the last years of steam. Through a number of short accounts the past comes vividly to life, via short stories about train crashes, pea-soup fogs, and fires going out.

9780752480435

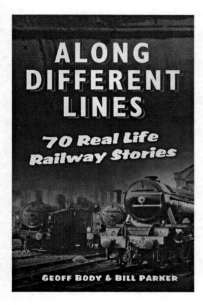

Along Different Lines
GEOFF BODY AND BILL PARKER

Running a railway is a complex business. There will always be surprises, often hilarious and sometimes serious. Here railway professionals recall notable incidents from across their careers on the railways, compiled by expert railwaymen and authors Geoff Body and Bill Parker. Including such bizarre events as coping with hurricanes, rogue locomotives and runaway wagons, PR successes and otherwise, the Brighton Belle, Flying Scotsman and *Mallard*, training course capers, a wino invasion, trackside antics and the birth of a prison.

9780752489155

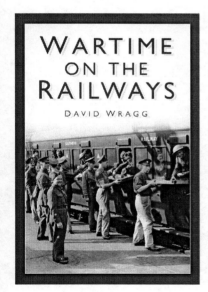

Wartime on the Railways
DAVID WRAGG

From the American Civil War onwards, railways have been an important aspect of war. *Wartime on the Railways* describes the part played by Britain's railways during the Second World War, dealing not simply with operational matters or the impact of enemy action on the railways, but also looking at financial arrangements, the part played by railway workshops in producing equipment for the military, the wartime experience of the railways' ships, with the narrative augmented by personal accounts from railwaymen, and women as the war years saw much change.

9780752486123

Visit our website and discover thousands of other History Press books.

www.thehistorypress.co.uk

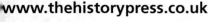

Lightning Source UK Ltd.
Milton Keynes UK
UKOW05f0235150115

244506UK00002B/13/P